How I Retired Successfully and Happily
and Happily
and Lived to Be 100

How I Retired Successfully
and Happily
and Lived to Be 100

5/9/18

A Memoir
by

Ira Neimark

To: CAMILIA & STUART

WITH MY VERY BEST WISHES

Ira

How I Retired Successfully and Happily and Lived to Be 100
Copyright © 2017 by Ira Neimark
Cover photograph

For further information contact:

GamePlan Press, Inc.
910 South George Mason Drive
Arlington,VA 222014

ISBN: 978-1-7321678-0-3

Dedicated to Janie Neimark Lewis

Acknowledgements

In addition to my wife Jackie, whose collection of newspaper articles featuring Bergdorf Goodman made this book possible; my daughter Robin Neimark Seegal, who helped with editing; my publisher, Maryann Karinch; David Moin, *Women's Wear Daily*; Arthur Sulzberger, *The New York Times*; William M. Holmes, President of Bonwit Teller and my "godfather"; my "godmother" and his secretary, Betty Vanderbilt; Beatrice Fox Auerbach, President of G. Fox & Co.; Leonard Johnson, President of Gladdings; Randy Stambaugh, President of B. Altman & Co.; Phil Hawley, CEO of Carter Hawley Hale; Leonard Lauder; Jeffry Aronsson, and Andrew Jennings, to name very few who helped make this wonderful story happen. There are too many others throughout my life who contributed mightily to be listed here. To you all, who know who you are, thank you, thank you.

Table of Contents

Author's Notes

The business of life is the acquisition of memories.
Mr. Carson, *Downton Abbey*

This book is made up of many memories leading up to my retirement. So many, in fact, that the book is divided into three parts.

Part 1
Remembering the adventurous days, during WWII, of being an Aviation Cadet in the Class of 43K. This was the first step toward achieving my first ambition in life, being a pilot in the U.S. Army Air Corps.

Part 2
My business career, which explains the concept by setting goals to be reached in life. Success can be achieved by always planning ahead.

Part 3
What to do when retired to extend the good habits that you enjoyed during your early years.

The reader may read any of the three parts, and possibly all three, in order to know my whole story. Or, just Part 3, my enjoyable priorities for a happy and successful retirement.

Introduction

When writing this memoir, I wanted to tell the story of how fortunate I have been to be successfully and happily retired, and to pass on this experience and advice on to others,—including what my priorities were to achieve a successful retirement.

My editors recommended that I include an outline of my family and an autobiography of my early years, leading up to my becoming the CEO of Bergdorf Goodman. This would help give the readers of this memoir a sense of the ingredients that helped me to reach that point. They further recommended that I include many of the newspaper clippings that chronicled Bergdorf Goodman's and my climb to success.

In any case, it is a lifelong story that may be helpful to those who take the time to read what it is that I have written.

During the research for the memoir, a major revelation came to me when I found my Pre Flight graduation book from the Army Aviation Cadet Class, 43K (December 1943). Heretofore, whenever I thought back to those exciting and challenging days, I always recalled my fellow cadets as vibrant and dynamic, and very young men.

Now, some seventy odd years later, as I read the names they signed in my graduation book, I came to the sudden realization that those who are still around are very old men. WWII was a major event in my life and theirs, I decided that they should not be forgotten.

These are the names of the Aviation Cadet Class of 43K, U.S. Army Air Corps. Maxwell Field, Montgomery, Alabama.

Alex Skalabam	Brooklyn, NY
Charles Taylor	
Chick Nasi *	Brooklyn, NY
Edw. G. McKinna	
Edward Johnson	Port Chester, NY
Edward Wildemutter	Reading, PA
Ernrst Morin *	Beverly, MA
Frank Lesconski	Riverhead, NY
George Bower	Boston, MA
George H. Penningten	
Glenn H. Royohn	Pennsylvania
H. A. Kaufman	Champlain, NY
Harold W. Rambusch	Huntington, L.I., NY
Haskell P. Rubin	Spring Valley, NY
Herman D. Weiner	New York, NY
Irv G. Carpine	
Irv. D. Thompson	
Irwin G. Nelson	New York, NY
Jack Mann	
John A. Jantz	Trenton, NJ
John G. Cunningham	
K. E. Brown	
Lionel P. Girard	Worcester, MA
Louis C. Marpil	Brooklyn, NY
M. O'Neil	
Mathew Wolofsky	Brooklyn, NY
Max E. Dixon	Springfield, OH
Monty Morrison	
Robert R Murray	Los Angeles, CA
Bernard Roth	Brooklyn, NY
Sidney L. Weiner	New York, NY
W. H. Major	Kansas City, MO
Walter E. Thain	Baltimore, MD

Walter Trout
Wllfred Scull
Wm. C. McCord   Illinois
Howard D. Nunn   Los Angeles, CA
Duloo R.Williams   Santa Monica, CA
Edward A. Stuckey   Niagara Falls, N
Willy Muntzer *

* Denotes a roommate. Also, please note I've left the names as they signed them.

     As young, accomplished pilot trainees, who had passed the stringent mental and physical examinations to get there, with their high spirits, they knew that they were special. We were.

Why I Wrote *How I Retired Successfully and Happily and Lived to Be 100*

The thought of writing this memoir came to me on my 95th birthday. Living to a healthy, productive and financially comfortable old age requires good family genes, a good and loving wife, a professional financial advisor, and a healthy and active lifestyle.

It was that birthday that made me think back to 1970, when I was leaving G. Fox & Co., in Hartford, to join B. Altman & Co., in New York. I realized then, at age 49, after working for ten years at G. Fox & Co., and leaving as executive vice president and general merchandise manager, that I had few retirement benefits of any significance.

I hoped that B. Altman & Co., my new employer, would have in place a retirement plan for the balance of my retail career.

They did have a plan, but my reliance upon it was short-lived as I was recruited by Carter Hawley Hale, five years later, to be the CEO of Bergdorf Goodman. CHH, as it was usually called, not only had a modern retirement plan, but, upon finalizing my employment contract, I found I had a very reasonable and adequate retirement package to look forward to in the future. In addition to the retirement plan, CHH, as an executive perk, paid for the services of a financial advisor.

In today's world, this may not be considered earth-shaking. But then approaching my early fifties, it allowed me to devote all my efforts to building Bergdorf Goodman to its rightful place as the leading fashion retailer. My financial ad - visor, Quarve Associates, in addition to watching my income, expenses and moderate investments, put together a retirement plan, with my main request, to have a plan allowing me and my wife Jackie to maintain our lifestyle after my retirement.

So far, at my 96th birthday, I am pleased to say, my retirement program has performed as planned.

Can everyone have the same goals and performance?

Of course not. Some people's retirements will far exceed my retirement goals. Others will fall far short and cause them considerable unhappiness and discomfort in their remaining years.

I am reminded of a merchandise manager, at G. Fox & Co., who upon reaching retirement age, came to my office saying to me, "I can't afford to retire. Can I stay on?" Of course he stayed on, and never retired.

This brief outline explains my financial planning and retirement objectives, as well as my recommendations for the younger generations following me. First of all, I found it is never too early in life to seek the advice and direction of a financial planner.

I have observed, over the years, many young executives, men and women, who do exceedingly well in their business careers, but come up far short in their personal financial planning.

I was determined, at age 50, this was not going to happen to me. I felt strongly about paying dues for an exercise program or a golf club for my physical health and enjoyment. It was equally as important to pay for having someone guide me for my financial health.

What Will I Do When I Retire?

There are a number of thoughts that came to my mind when my retirement was approaching.

One: I am reminded of my old boss, Randy Stambaugh, president of B. Altman & Co., saying after he retired, "I don't know what I am doing, but I am busy every day."

Two: I remember a wife saying, "We married for better or for worse, not for lunch." Lunch is no big deal. Ask any widow. I have an enjoyable lunch with my wife every day, by the way. (Except golf days.)

Three: I had an experience, within my first week of re - tirement that made me determined not to sit around and grow old.

My younger daughter, Robin, invited me to drive up with my 4-year-old granddaughter Hallie, to the Sea Museum in Norwalk, Connecticut. While driving there and during my tour, then returning home, I was visibly shaken. Up until that day, as CEO of Bergdorf Goodman, I had many business decisions to make. All of a sudden it had stopped. Was I going to spend the rest of my life visiting aquariums and museums with my grandchildren?

I then decided that those experiences I had found enjoyable during my younger years could, and would be, my priorities for my retirement.

Before laying out these priorities, I thought back over my lifetime and my business career to recall what it was that got me to this point of having a successful, happy and healthy retirement. The following is a brief biography of the *Career, Coincidence and Luck* that got me to that point.

After my priorities for retirement, is a section of newspaper clippings regarding the progress of bringing Bergdorf Goodman to its place as the leading fashion specialty store in New York City. In 1991, that included my participation in building the largest Men's Store on Fifth Avenue.

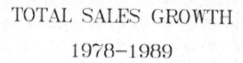

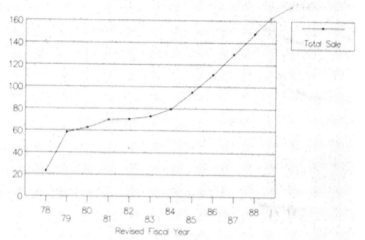

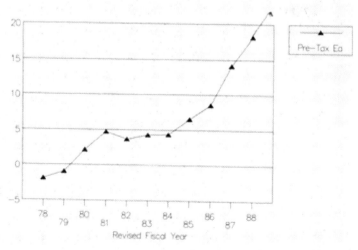

Career, Coincidence and Luck
The Autobiography in Brief

L ooking back on my career, I had a strong feeling that co-incidence and luck played a major role in helping me to achieve the many goals in my life.

I have often thought that life, in a number of ways, is like a large pinball machine. The ball bounces where it will; sometimes, helped with a little push, the ball can be moved in the desired direction.

This belief, using my pinball theory, brings to mind a good number of coincidences. It would seem with those coincidences, a lot of luck and the ball bouncing in the right direction have brought about my successful business career.

During The Great Depression, when I was sixteen years old, I had to drop out of Erasmus Hall high school to earn a living to help my mother. This was necessary, due to the tragedy of losing my father to an automobile accident when I was eleven years old.

During that time, my mother held our family—my two brothers and me—together by going to work as a salesperson at Stern's Department Store, on 42nd Street, where the Grace office building stands today.

I must admit, even though I was the president and the valedictorian of my graduating class at PS 181, and the president of my freshman class at Erasmus Hall High School, my grades, particularly in Latin, indicated that I was not going to be a candidate for a Rhodes Scholarship.

With high school not contributing to our immediate needs at home, I left school to find any job in order to help out during The Great Depression. A tragic and trying time, not only for us, but also almost everyone.

My first jobs, delivering laundry then groceries, were not generating enough income to make either of these jobs worthwhile. However, three, history-making experiences that happened during that period have stayed in my mind over these many years.

One day, during the summer of 1938, when delivering groceries, I had a case of beer to be delivered to a husband and wife who lived in our apartment building. A case of beer in those days was a heavy wooden crate with twelve bottles. When I deposited the beer in their apartment, I saw a large framed picture of Adolf Hitler on their living room wall. I was a bit startled, knowing this was the beginning of something that was not good.

The second occurred when, while pushing my laundry wagon, I saw the Hindenburg dirigible fly over Prospect Park, on its way to its demise. It would blow up and be destroyed at Lakehurst, New Jersey. The date was May 6, 1937.

I was still delivering groceries when on September 21, 1938, a very strong wind picked up enough for branches to begin falling from trees. Before the storm grew much worse, I returned home to learn that this was to be called the Great Hurricane of 1938. I decided my apprenticeship of delivering laundry and groceries was over. Now on to a real job.

Why, when I was 16 years old, did I apply for work at the Hamilton Employment Agency, in the financial district? Was I sent there by someone, or was it just luck? I cannot, as much as I have tried to, remember what or who it was that recommended that I apply for a job at that employment agency.

In everyone's lifetime a circumstance sets in motion a life-changing situation that alters the direction of that person's life. It could be moving to another city, marriage, job change, or any number of occurrences. This, without my knowing it, was my life-changing opportunity.

Banks in the financial district used the Hamilton Agency to hire employees. Hence, after sitting around for a couple of days, I was sent to the Hanover Bank and Trust Company to interview for the job of a runner.

In those days, a runner was a uniformed office boy with the additional responsibility of delivering financial documents to other banks. This required carrying a large brief case that was locked and handcuffed to the runner. For a few weeks, I enjoyed my new job.

Unfortunately, when applying for the job, I was required to answer a number of questions on the job application, including one on the name of my high school and the date of my graduation. Naturally, I put down Erasmus Hall and picked a date of graduation.

Shortly after, I was called to the bank's employment office and told that the information on graduating from Erasmus was not correct, so I could no longer be employed by The Hanover Bank and Trust Company.

That situation ended my banking career. Still, because of that misstep, a new career was waiting for me.

How could I be so lucky to lose my two-week job at the Manufacturers Hanover Bank and Trust Co., by their finding out that I was not a graduate of Erasmus Hall High School?

Hamilton didn't seem concerned and sent me on for an interview to Bonwit Teller, 721 Fifth Avenue, for a Christmas job as a pageboy in their 721 Christmas Club.

The 721 Club was an area in the store exclusively for men shoppers during the Christmas season. I was required to wear a Philip Morris-type page boy uniform, and welcome men to the club.

Was it a coincidence that the president of Bonwit Teller, William M. Holmes, was also a high school dropout and had immigrated as a young boy from Ireland? Bill Holmes as he was called by close friends and business associates, identified with my being a dropout, and became my mentor throughout most of my retail career.

If Bill Holmes had not been made the president of Bonwit Teller, there would not have been a 721 Club and no need for a pageboy.

Fast forward: In 1982, when I was the CEO of Bergdorf Goodman, Donald Trump invited me to lunch at 21. Mr. Trump asked for my assistance. He wanted me to appear before the New York City Planning Commission, to give Bergdorf Goodman's approval to build Trump Tower on the Bonwit Teller 721 5th Avenue site. Which of course I did. It was to Bergdorf Goodman's advantage then to have Trump Tower uptown—better than downtown, nearer to Saks 5th Avenue.

What a difference forty plus years makes. Here I was in 1938, hired as page boy for the 721 Club; now, in 1982, as CEO of Bergdorf Goodman, I was giving my approval for Trump Tower to be built on the Bonwit Teller site. As a reward, I asked Donald Trump to give me the door handle on Bonwit Teller's 56th Street door entrance—where I began my retail career as assistant to the doorman. He did. It sits on my desk, to this day, reminding me of my humble beginning as a retailer.

I must admit, I was always a bit sentimental, and I also believed in symbolism. Before the actual destruction of the Bonwit Teller building took place, I entered through a side door and walked up the back staircase to the fourth floor.

I stood in the middle of the floor, in the exact location where, 44 years earlier, I stood as a pageboy for Bonwit's 721 Club.

I reflected back to all that had happened to me, during those years, and considered myself as one very fortunate individual.

An aside: When Donald Trump won the presidential election, Trump Tower became the focal point of his and others coming and going. So much so, TV cameras were always turned on the entrance. Pictures on the TV reminded me when I was the assistant to the doorman at Bonwit Teller. One of my responsibilities was to relieve the Fifth Avenue doorman for his lunch hour. I was to stand at the main entrance, which is now Trump Tower's entrance.

During one of those days, a taxi cab pulled up, I opened the door, and out jumped a man with a large mustache turned up at both ends. He went into the store. A few minutes later, he crashed a bathtub from one of his window displays through the Fifth Avenue window. It seems, someone, without his permission, changed the mannequin wearing a fur coat, standing in a matching fur lined bathtub.

It was Salvador Dali.

Again, the TV photos reminded me of my hailing taxis and opening doors for customers, as they arrived by car, and fancy limousine. In those days, some really wealthy customers drove up with their chauffeured Rolls Royces and, often, a footman as well.

All this activity added tips to my income during those difficult financial days.

After Donald Trump won the election, maintaining his office in Trump Tower, it is interesting to look back on those experiences. I now see those positions, where I was once stationed, have become a major landmark in Donald Trump's presidency. Where I stood as a young man in front of an upscale department store, there are now armed guards outside the gold-framed, revolving door of the building.

THE BOOKIE'S ASSISTANT

In January 1939, after serving as the page boy at Bonwit Teller's Christmas 721 Club, I was promoted to assistant to the doorman, at Bonwit Teller's 56th Street entrance. This position presented many financial opportunities, in addition to my small salary, and tips for hailing taxi cabs (and would you believe, checking customers' umbrellas on rainy days?).

Also another source of income became available.

After the Whitneys, Vanderbilts and others had visited their stables at Belmont Race Track in the morning, they came to Bonwit's Beauty Salon in the early afternoon. Naturally, the employees in the salon asked the racing stable owners, what tips on their horses did they have for them today? Win, place or show, for their horses? When the tips were given, the bets were sent down to the 56th street door to be placed with George, the local bookie.

I found that part of my job description was to place the bets with George, and off I went to a phone booth at a drug store across Fifth Avenue.

This was a scene out of *Guys and Dolls*. There was George, in the phone booth, hat on the back of his head, receiver stuck on his shoulder, calling in the bets in as I was handing in Bonwit's bets.

My payment was 5 cents on every dollar placed.

The income was well received, until George asked me to cover the neighborhood for him. I discussed this proposal with my mother. Her response in addition to giving me a whack on my rear end: "I didn't bring you up to be a bookie."

Thus ended my career as a bookie.

WINNING THE IRISH SWEEPSTAKES

Going back a number of years, to the early 1930s, I had another horse racing experience that I never forgot.

During the Great Depression, Irish hospitals in order to raise funds to support their hospitals, had lotteries called The Irish Sweepstakes. The winners in those days would make headlines in all the newspapers. I don't recall the major winnings, but somewhere around $5,000,000 seems right. In today's dollars, about $90,000,000. There were lower amounts based on which horses would win, place or show, (first, second and third)

One day, around 1934/5, when my brothers and I returned home from school, our housekeeper, Marie, who didn't speak English very well, said something about a telegram and sweeps.

We looked at the telegram from Ireland. I will never forget. It read, "Congratulations, you are consolation winners in the Grand National Irish Sweepstakes. 100 pounds."

We totally ignored the word consolation, and called my mother on the phone where she was visiting some friends, and said, "We won the Irish Sweepstakes." We heard screaming at the other end of the phone. My mother raced home, in her lavender Marmon to see the telegram. We were puzzled about the word consolation winners, since the newspapers never mentioned them; hence our believing, or wanting to believe we won the grand prize.

I recall going next door to our neighbor, Mr. Herman, a lawyer, and asking him his opinion about the telegram. He confirmed unfortunately, the amount was, as stated, 100 pounds. About a five hundred dollars. Of course, we were greatly dis - appointed, but glad that we won something.

The moral of this story is don't count your chickens before they hatch, or always talk to a lawyer first.

TO AND FROM BONWIT TELLER

Bonwit Teller was a wonderful experience, bringing me a lot of luck in beginning a wonderful career. It would seem like the ball bounced in the right direction, first being sent to The Hamilton Agency, then losing my job at the bank, then being sent on to Bonwit Teller, for my life long career in retailing.

Unfortunately, after Bill Holmes retired in 1947 the change in Bonwit Teller's ownership and management, made me decide to look for another job after thirteen wonderful years at Bonwit Teller, with three years out serving with the Army Air Corps during WWII.

Before signing up with US Air Corps, in July 1942, I was involved in Civilian Defense, becoming an air raid warden in 1939, and then joining the New York National Guard in 1940.

The Armory was located at Park Avenue and 34th Street. Long gone. We did our drills at night in the neighborhood. We left for Fort Drum in upstate New York that summer.

Marching up Park Avenue to Grand Central Station, bands playing, flags flying, people cheering, I could see why military parades made people enthusiastically patriotic.

There was a Catch 22 involved in my wanting to join the Air Corps. It seems that when enlisting in the National Guard, I signed papers for a term of enlistment. However, patriotism being what it was in those days, the NYNG, released me to join the Air Corps.

Those three years, starting in 1943 as an aviation cadet at Maxwell Field, ended on Saipan in what was called The Pacific Theater at the end of the war in 1945. My returning to the

States in February 1946 is covered in my first book, *Crossing Fifth Avenue to Bergdorf Goodman.*

Leaving Bonwit Teller in 1951, after all those wonderful years, was difficult: starting at Bonwit's 721 Club, assistant to the doorman, office boy to the president, stock boy, unit control clerk, returning from the war, rehired by Bonwit Teller for the merchandise office, assistant to the president and finally Bonwit's blouse buyer. This was a career of learning that served me successfully throughout my business career. For example, my short time as a blouse buyer showed me that selecting merchandise was not my strongest talent. Selecting people was.

The demise of Bonwit Teller began with Hoving Corporation's ownership, specifically Walter Hoving's decision to open many Bonwit Teller branch stores. The first two major branches, one in Boston, followed a year or two later by a store in Chicago were a failed and fatal business strategy.

This disastrous business lesson, learned by me, was enormously beneficial to my career years later, when I became the CEO of Bergdorf Goodman.

Before I became the CEO of Bergdorf Goodman, Bergdorf's first branch store in White Plains, New York was a failure. This failure convinced CHH, the owners, to convert the Bergdorf Goodman store to Neiman Marcus. Neiman's was in the branch store business, as both Bergdorf Goodman and Bonwit Teller, two prominent Fifth Avenue high fashion specialty stores, were not.

It was time for me to move on from Bonwit Teller. This once wonderful store, provided me with what I consider better than, or at the very least, equal to a business school education.

What was it that made me accept a job as a divisional merchandise manager at Gladdings, a fashion specialty store in Providence, Rhode Island?

My following Bill Holmes from Bonwit Teller to James McCreery, a mid-level department store on 34th Street in NYC, as a blouse buyer, was a mistake for me as well as for him.

McCreery stood for nothing other than having everyday merchandise. This was one of the first of the many department stores to go out of business during the fifties and sixties. After one year I decided McCreery was not for me.

Once again an employment agency changed the direction of my life. Betty Vanderbilt, Bill Holmes' secretary, recommended that I meet Alice Groves, an executive recruiter.

I consider Betty Vanderbilt my fairy godmother, who helped to guide my early business career.

The Alice Groves agency then recommended that I apply for openings as a merchandise manager at two fashion stores— The Blum Store in Philadelphia and Gladdings in Providence, Rhode Island.

After visiting both stores and again a recommendation from Bill Holmes, I joined Gladdings in 1951.

A year after joining Gladdings, I met Jackie Myers. The ball really bounced in the right direction then. The consequence and good luck of our meeting, with recommendations from many good friends, has been a lifetime of a loving marriage and raising our marvelous family.

Bonwit Teller taught me the basics of the fashion business. I learned Yankee merchandising at Gladdings.

One of the great advantages being employed by Gladdings was their membership in The Frederick Atkins Buying Office. The members of the Atkins stores were then the gilt edge of retailers—stores such as G. Fox & Co., B. Altman & Co., John Wanamaker, Woodward and Lothrop, Broadway Stores (later Carter Hawley Hale), etc.

Except for Dillard's, every well-known Atkins retailer listed in 1972 has disappeared from the retail scene, many due to competition from large shopping malls, discount stores, heavy taxes passing on family ownership, and not planning for the future. This was previous to the Internet, of course, which would have made them disappear sooner rather than later.

My being exposed to the top executives of these stores, created the opportunity, later on, for my being appointed executive vice president, general merchandise manager of both G.Fox & Co., and B. Altman & Co., and finally, the CEO of Bergdorf Goodman.,

How did I become lucky enough to have the opportunity of presenting, at a Frederic Atkins store principles meeting, my merchandise plan that got the attention of Beatrice Fox Auerbach, the owner of G. Fox & Co. in Hartford Connecticut?

My first year at Gladdings was not an outstanding suc- cess.

On one of my first dates with Jackie, I mentioned my frustration with my position at Gladdings, which made me consider moving on to another job offer. When Jackie became visibly upset, I decided to work out my initial problems at Gladdings and fortunately went on to success, becoming Gladdings' executive vice president and general merchandise manager.

That was the first of many important decisions of my career, where Jackie was the deciding influence.

It was at Gladdings where I developed my Unit Weeks of Supply Inventory procedure.

Managing inventories was always a mystery to me as it has been for all retailers over many years. (And still is.)

My procedure was so successful at Gladdings that it brought inventories into proper relationships with sales, thus greatly improving gross profits. I was then invited to present my Unit Weeks of Supply procedure at a Frederick Atkins store principles meeting, at the Greenbrier Resort.

Of all the fifty or so principals present, only one store president asked me to present my inventory management procedure to her executives. This was the legendary Beatrice Fox Auerbach, the owner of G. Fox and Co. in Hartford Connecticut. In fact, Mrs. Auebach's invitation was really an offer for me to join G. Fox, as assistant to the general merchandise manager, who would be retiring in a few years.

Providence, where Gladdings was located, was where I not only had the good fortune of marrying Jackie and having our two wonderful daughters, Janie and Robin, but it was also the beginning of a successful retail career.

In 1951, I was a stranger from New York City joining a real, old line Yankee retailer. After eight years, I had moved up from a divisional merchandise manager to executive vice president, general merchandise and godfather to the president's grandson.

Fortunately, my successful performance at Gladdings got the attention of other Atkins store principals. The letters sent to me, by the president, chairman of the board and the board of directors, have been a great source of satisfaction to me. Hence, the invitation, in 1959, for me to join G.Fox &Co., as assistant to the general merchandise manager.

My career at G. Fox, for close to ten years, was one of the most satisfying business experiences of my retail career. After five years, I was promoted to executive vice president, general merchandise manager of G. Fox & Co.

Beatrice Fox Auerbach was inspirational. From her I learned how to run a store geared to customer satisfaction as the highest priority. In addition, my Unit Weeks of Supply program was used throughout the apparel departments, with great success. Once again, I gained the attention of other major retailers.

I mention eight years of satisfaction; my last two years at G. Fox were the unhappiest of my long career.

In 1968 Beatrice Fox Auerbach sold G. Fox to The May Department Stores. The management of May Co. had a completely different approach and retail concept of how to handle executives, as well as executives, than Beatrice Auerbach had.

She died two years after the sale. I was so uncomfortable working for the May Co. that I was preparing to leave.

If nothing else, Beatrice Fox Auerbach, taught me the importance of the customer as the key to success. No matter what the business. I often repeat her mantra, "Get out of your office; the customer is on the selling floor, not in your office." Don't ever forget it!

With that in mind, I'd like to offer some classic advice—and I don't know the source—on "What is a customer?" A version of this has always been on my desk to remind me and my organization of the following:

- A customer is the most important person in our business.
- A customer is not dependent on us. We are dependent on the customer.
- A customer is not an interruption of our work. A customer is the purpose of it.
- A customer does us a favor when coming in. We are not doing customers a favor by waiting on them.

After eight years of being employed with a successful career at G. Fox & Co., the ball seemed to bounce in the wrong direction when G. Fox was sold to The May Department Stores.

My last two years at G. Fox showed me the difference between a family run store *versus* a corporation that is mainly concerned with the bottom line. It showed that a management style mainly concerned with customer satisfaction had greater results going to the bottom line. The results of the May company concept have in many cases been a disaster for stores concentrating on the bottom line, instead of concentrating on customer service—with customer service being defined as the customer being recognized as a valued asset—and delivering, when, how, and what it was that their customers wanted.

The ball bounced in the right direction when I felt it was time for me to leave G. Fox before the May Co. made that move for me.

The coincidence of B. Altman & Co. looking for a general merchandise manager at the same time that I decided to leave G. Fox was again great luck and timing. B. Altman & Co. deciding to hire me, as their general merchandise manager, was another great opportunity, as well as a great coincidence during an unsettling time for me.

My returning to New York and spending five years at B. Altman & Co. on Fifth Avenue was another enjoyable high-light in my business career.

On a personal note, Jackie, and my daughters Janie and Robin, were thrilled with the prospect of living so close to the big city.

B. Altman was a wonderful store, and the senior executives were wonderful as well. Here too, as at G. Fox, the customer was paramount. I was very much at home.

Changing B. Altman from a very successful home furnishing store with a reputation for not being an up-to-date fashion store for women and men was a fascinating challenge. Hiring and appointing the right people in order to bring the store up to date was a successful step. Major fashion lines were featured. A major new cosmetic department was built, as well as a significant move of the men's departments to the main Fifth Avenue floor. Slowly, but surely, the store was being recog - nized—not only by customers, but the fashion press also began paying attention and B. Altman was on its way.

THE MOVE TO BERGDORF GOODMAN

Carter Hawley Hale buying Neiman Marcus in 1967 and then buying Bergdorf Goodman in 1972 was, for me, another remarkable case of luck, coincidence and timing.

Bergdorf Goodman's unsuccessful opening of their first branch store in White Plains, New York set up the pinball and coincidences to come together for my next opportunity.

Good luck and coincidence happened, once again, when CHH decided to bring to Bergdorf Goodman a new, experienced CEO.

The pinball once again bounced in my direction when Phil Hawley, CEO of Carter Hawley, asked Leonard Lauder who would he recommend to be the CEO of Bergdorf Goodman? Career, coincidence and luck all came together once again when Phil Hawley followed Leonard Lauder's advice, and hired me to be the CEO of Bergdorf Goodman. The rest is seventeen years of an enjoyable, successful business career.

It was at Bergdorf Goodman that an unprecedented opportunity was presented to me.

Here was this magnificent store located diagonally across Fifth Avenue from Bonwit Teller, where I was brought up, waiting to be awakened.

Bergdorf Goodman was under the Goodman family ownership, first under Edwin Goodman, then his son Andrew.

The business started in lower New York, as a custom tailor shop early in the 1900s. Herman Bergdorf was the owner, then Edwin Goodman, first his partner, bought out Mr. Bergdorf.

With several moves uptown, finally, the Bergdorf Good man building on Fifth Avenue became the headquarters for what was recognized as the height of Women's Fashions.

Andrew Goodman, taking over after his father's death in 1953, maintained the elegance and high fashion reputation that the store was known for. The sales volume when I was appointed president and chief executive officer was stable at about thirty-eight million dollars a year.

I mention maintained: Andrew Goodman did a magnifi cent job of maintaining the reputation of the high fashion business. He introduced, as well, the very successful Miss Bergdorf department. However, in the early 1970s a very important and exciting new fashion development was taking place, and bringing tremendous success to Bergdorf Goodman's competitors, Henri Bendel, Bloomingdales, Saks Fifth Avenue and Barneys, downtown.

New fashion designers had emerged in Italy, such as Fendi, Armani, and many more; in France, Eve Saint Laurent, Chanel and Dior; in the US, Ralph Lauren, Calvin Klein, Donna Karan, Geoffrey Beene. They were all striking out on their own with great success.

Unfortunately, Bergdorf Goodman buyers were either not interested in these new names in fashion, or satisfied with their own recourses. This was the great opportunity waiting for me when I was appointed CEO. With our fashion office headed by Dawn Mello and our finances headed by Steve Elkin, we were off and running.

Initially, these exciting new fashion houses who were selling to Bergdorf Goodman's competitors, were hesitant to sell to Bergdorf's, the ultra-conservative fashion store. It took great effort to convince Fendi to sell their leather goods, furs, and ready to wear, exclusively, all under one roof, to Bergdorf Goodman. When Fendi came on board, slowly but surely, one fashion designer after another agreed to sell their collections to Bergdorf Goodman. We were now on our way. Adding these and other fashion designers not only increased sales and profits, it brought Bergdorf Goodman back as the fashion leader on Fifth Avenue.

   The initial business concept was for Bergdorf Goodman to open branch stores, the same as Neiman Marcus. However, with the failure of Bergdorf's first branch in White Plains, New York, the branch store strategy was dropped in order to concentrate on the hidden gold mine of Bergdorf Goodman on Fifth Avenue.

   Today, Bergdorf Goodman's Women's and Men's store sales are estimated to be close to one billion dollars.

   The graphs show that after three years of bringing top fashion houses to Bergdorfs, sales and profits increased dra - matically.

   With expenses and inventories being monitored and controlled by Steve Elkin, fashion direction and leadership by Dawn Mello, public relations and advertising by Susie Butterfield, window and interior displays by Angela Patterson, and last, but most important, human resources and training directed by Marita O'Dea, we had a team of highly experienced professionals making outstanding sales and profits possible. From this highly professional group I coined the phrase, "Pros hire Pros, Dummies hire Dummies."

   My books *Crossing Fifth Avenue to Bergdorf Goodman*; *The Rise of Fashion and Lessons Learned at Bergdorf Goodman*; *A Retailer's Lifetime of Lessons Learned* (a handbook for present and future young entrepreneurs); and *The Rise of Bergdorf Goodman and The Fall of Bonwit Teller (*which was written in 2015) have all the stories and details of how this very successful retail venture came about.

Abraham Schuel, Hortense Odlum, William M. Holmes Treasurer, President, and General Manager, respectively, of Bonwit Teller. The cake behind them was a model of the Bonwit Teller building in 1937.

Bonwit Teller 1938
Courtesy The Department Store Museum

The building, 721 Fifth Avenue, was replaced in the 1980s
by Trump Tower.

2017 photo courtesy of *The New York Times*

1951 Photo of Bonwit Teller buyers and Sara Pennoyer advertising manager, one of my early supporters, had a party congratulating me on becoming the merchandise manager of Gladdings.

Sales people from my blouse department

The Decline of Bonwit Teller: Did Time Pass Retailer By?

By ISADORE BARMASH

1990

Twenty years ago, Bonwit Teller and Saks Fifth Avenue, two of the nation's most celebrated fashion retailers catering to affluent customers, were roughly equivalent in size and approach.

But today, as businesses, they are worlds apart. Saks, owned since 1974 by a British company, has become the nation's prime seller of clothing to affluent women, has greatly expanded its men's clothing lines and is now one of the nation's most profitable retailers. Bonwit this week began going-out-of-business sales as its losses under its Australian parent company became insurmountable.

Lack of Consistency Seen

The unhappy story of Bonwit's demise, analysts said, is a case of a retailer that first lost its edge in marketing and then became a repeated takeover target, with each new owner shifting strategies. Customers, understandably confused, fled to other stores. And so Bonwit's once-profitable marketing formula of catering mainly to affluent, fashion-conscious women was squandered.

"I don't mean to be unkind," said Marvin J. Rothenberg, head of the retail marketing consulting firm bearing his name, "but Bonwit Teller was dead for years, only no one buried it."

The Pyramid Companies of Syracuse, which bought the Bonwit name and the leases on two Bonwit stores, said it would heed the lessons of the retailer's decline. Pyramid plans to en-

courage a new top management team to focus sharply on profits, partly by giving the executives a 50 percent stake in the business.

Industry analysts said that Bonwit's problems were magnified by the operational and marketing changes brought about as at least 10 management teams altered the company with their own agendas. By comparison, Saks had

Continued on Page 32, Column 4

Bonwit Teller is holding a going-out-of-business sale at its flagship store at East 57th Street in Manhattan and shoppers went bargain hunting yesterday amid the display cases.

Did Time Pass Bonwit Teller By?

Continued From Page 1

three top-management shuffles in the same period, and they kept the chain's policy consistent. They also drove Saks's sales to six times that of Bonwit's — more than $1 billion, compared with $160 million — and kept the stores profitable while Bonwit suffered intermittent losses.

Both Bonwit and Saks were put up for sale several months ago, but for very different reasons. Bonwit drew no bidders, while the stores alluring Saks attracted eight, leading to strong expectations than it will soon have new owners.

Behind the Sale Signs

The Hooker Corporation, the Australian developer that bought both Bonwit and B. Altman, went into Chapter 11 bankruptcy in August and put Bonwit on the block to raise cash. Last week a Federal bankruptcy judge approved Hooker's plan to liquidate most of the Bonwit stores. As a result, there was a sharp cutback in the number of stores, to 4 from 16, effectively putting the other 12 out of business.

As managements and strategies kept shifting, the customers fled.

For its part, Saks's owner, B.A.T Industries of London, is selling off Saks, along with Marshall Field & Company and other American retail entities, to focus on its core tobacco business and forestall a hostile takeover by Sir James Goldsmith, the British financier.

'It Was a Great Company'

Rival retailers express sympathy but are often caustic about the reasons for Bonwit's downfall.

"I started with Bonwit and it was a great company many years ago," said Ira Neimark, chairman and chief executive of Bergdorf Goodman. "But the lack of consistent management is one of the biggest reasons why Bonwit lost its way."

Paul Leblang, senior vice president of marketing for Saks Fifth Avenue, said: "Bonwit's ultimately failed to satisfy its customers and no longer was the 'destination' store. If you don't project yourself in a consistent way, you lose your spot on the positioning ladder."

Mr. Leblang added, "Consumers

didn't quite know what Bonwit's had anymore."

It is now up to Pyramid, whose store leases are in Boston and Buffalo, to give Bonwit a second life of sorts. Pyramid says it will also seek to replace the flagship store being closed in Trump Tower in Manhattan with another one on Fifth Avenue. Two other Bonwit stores, in Hooker shopping malls in Cincinnati and Columbia, S.C., will continue to operate under a license from Pyramid.

Robert Congel, Pyramid's managing partner, said he hoped to revive Bonwit by "positioning a new management team we have selected, by offering its four members almost half of the business, by giving them a debt-free company and eventually a new flagship."

Pyramid has built most of its 16 malls in the Northeast by offering partnerships to experts in finance, legal affairs, mall leasing and construction. Pyramid typically retains a 50 percent stake in those centers.

'Total Control' Sought

Mr. Congel said Pyramid would not restrict Bonwit stores to just company-owned malls, of which 17 new ones are in development. He said plans called for new Bonwit stores in "appropriate, upscale locations in such cities as Philadelphia and New York." He added, "It's wise to open at least one new Bonwit a year but we want to have total control."

The company was started by Paul J. Bonwit in the 1890's when he opened a small shop at Sixth Avenue and 18th Street selling fine women's apparel and exclusive designs. In 1898, he formed a partnership with Edmund D. Teller.

Bonwit was acquired by the Allied Stores Corporation in 1879 from Genesco Inc., and Allied seemed to give it the expansion and confidence that conquering retail executives say it deserved.

Allied moved the flagship store to Trump Tower and it seemed that after years of static ownership Bonwit might finally thrive. But in 1986, Allied was acquired in a hostile takeover by the Campeau Corporation, the Canadian real estate developer.

"One of the first things Robert Campeau told me in 1986 was that Bonwit had to be sold," said William Ruben, who was chairman and chief executive of Bonwit from 1983 through March 1988.

Walter K. Levy, a retail-marketing consultant, said: "Genesco bought Bonwit for prestige. Allied bought it to go upscale and Hooker bought it for anchors for its medium-income malls." But Bonwit was a high-priced retailer that did not fit into some of the new Hooker malls, he said.

Even under Allied, said Jerome Chazen, chairman of Liz Claiborne

Inc., a leading women's apparel maker, Bonwit surrendered its prime focus. "To Allied, it was regarded only as a small, insignificant entity," he added.

But Mr. Ruben said: "I thought that Bonwit should be expanded into existing markets, like New York, Chicago and Philadelphia, where there could be economies of scale in advertising and distribution. But Hooker took a fine, upscale retailer and put it in the wrong markets."

In the summer of 1989, however, Hooker found itself with little money even after selling Bonwit's accounts receivables to the GE Capital Corporation.

Recalling that Bonwit in the late 1980's had an enviable 10 percent operating profit margin, Mr. Levy, the New York consultant who had also worked for Bonwit, attributed the gains to the introduction of designer clothes at the chain by Mildred Custin, then Bonwit's chairman.

"But as Bonwit's began to flounder," Mr. Levy said, "it lost the sharp elbows that Saks Fifth Avenue had. Without that or a more critical mass, it meant that Bonwit couldn't get its deliveries on time nor enough exclusives to make it stand out."

FREDERICK ATKINS, INC.
11 WEST 42nd STREET, NEW YORK, N. Y. 10036
564-0300

ADAM, MELDRUM & ANDERSON CO., INC.	Buffalo, New York	14205
GEORGE ALLEN, INC.	Germantown, Philadelphia, Pa.	19144
B. ALTMAN & CO.	New York, New York	10016
AUERBACH COMPANY	Salt Lake City, Utah	84110
THE BROADWAY	Los Angeles, California	90031
CARLISLE'S	Ashtabula, Ohio	44004
T. A. CHAPMAN COMPANY	Milwaukee, Wisconsin	53202
CLELAND SIMPSON CO.	Scranton, Pennsylvania	18503
D & L STORES	New Britain, Conn.	06050
DENBY'S INC.	Troy, New York	12180
DILLARD'S DEPARTMENT STORES, INC.		
BROWN DUNKIN CO.	Tulsa, Oklahoma	74102
DILLARD'S	San Antonio, Texas	78213
PFEIFER-BLASS	Little Rock, Arkansas	72203
M. EPSTEIN, INC.	Morristown, New Jersey	07960
GARFINCKEL'S	Washington, D. C.	20004
GLADDING'S INC.	Providence, Rhode Island	02901
HOCHSCHILD, KOHN	Baltimore, Maryland	21201
D. H. HOLMES COMPANY, LTD.	New Orleans, Louisiana	70160
J. B. IVEY & COMPANY		
IVEY'S CHARLOTTE	Charlotte, North Carolina	28201
IVEY'S GREENVILLE	Greenville, South Carolina	29602
IVEY'S RALEIGH	Raleigh, North Carolina	27602
IVEY'S ORLANDO	Orlando, Florida	32802
IVEY'S JACKSONVILLE	Jacksonville, Florida	32202
THE KILLIAN COMPANY	Cedar Rapids, Iowa	52406
LIBERTY HOUSE — California	San Francisco, Calif.	94108
LUCKEY, PLATT & CO.	Poughkeepsie, New York	12601
HARRY S. MANCHESTER, INC.	Madison, Wisconsin	53701
MARTIN'S	Brooklyn, New York	11201
McCURDY & COMPANY, INC.	Rochester, New York	14604
McRAE'S	Jackson, Mississippi	39209
MILLER BROTHERS COMPANY	Chattanooga, Tennessee	37401
MILLER & RHOADS	Richmond, Virginia	23217
MILLER'S, INC.	Knoxville, Tennessee	37901
MONNIG'S	Fort Worth, Texas	76101
PIZITZ	Birmingham, Alabama	35203
PORTEOUS MITCHELL & BRAUN CO.	Portland, Maine	04101
RHODES		
RHODES (California)	Oakland, California	94612
RHODES, (Southwest)	Phoenix, Arizona	85010
RHODES (Northwest)	Portland, Oregon	97205
THE SHEPARD CO.	Providence, Rhode Island	02903
THE ROBERT SIMPSON COMPANY, LTD.	Toronto, Canada	
R. H. STEARNS COMPANY	Boston, Massachusetts	02111
ALBERT STEIGER, INC.	Springfield, Massachusetts	01101
PAUL STEKETEE & SONS	Grand Rapids, Michigan	49501
CHAS. A. STEVENS & CO.	Chicago, Illinois	60602
STONE & THOMAS	Wheeling, West Virginia	26003
TOWNSEND & WALL COMPANY	St. Joseph, Missouri	64501
TRIMINGHAM BROTHERS, LTD.	Hamilton, Bermuda	
JOHN WANAMAKER — PHILA.	Philadelphia, Pennsylvania	19014
JOHN WANAMAKER — LIBERTY STREET	New York, New York	10038
WEINSTOCK'S	Sacramento, California	95803
ZOLLINGER-HARNED CO.	Allentown, Penn.	18101

Except for Dillard's, every well-known Atkins retailer
listed here in 1972 has disappeared from the retail scene.

My successful performance at Gladdings got the attention of other Atkins store principles. The letters sent to me, by the president, chairman of the board and the board of directors has been a great source of satisfaction to me.

Gladding's

SINCE 1766 PROVIDENCE RHODE ISLAND

OFFICE OF THE PRESIDENT

March 17, 1959

Mr. Ira Neimark
54 Belknap Road
West Hartford, Conn.

Dear Ira:

It is a pleasure to enclose a check which was voted at our Directors' Meeting, Saturday.

I am sure you would have been pleased to hear the nice comments made about you and the regret expressed that you had to leave our Store. It goes without saying how I feel! You will note that we have only deducted the P.A.Y.G., which is a requirement.

I used a lot of your material in my President's Report as you detailed out a rather clear resume of our fiscal 1958. The Board was pleased with our showing and voted an increased dividend based on our stronger financial position.

Mildred and I will try to visit you some fine Spring day.

Give our best to Jackie.

Cordially

L.E.Johnson/i
Enc.ck.

Hi! Congratulations on this, if you know what I mean!
m y o

The ground-breaking ceremony of Gladdings second branch store

BUSINESS CAREERS, INC.

347 Fifth Avenue, New York 16, N.Y.

February 26th
1 9 6 5

Mr. Ira Neimark
54 Balknap Road
West Hartford, Connecticut

Dear Ira:

I guess I can't help myself when it
comes to thinking of you in relation to
interesting jobs.

Although I am well aware that you are in
a fabulous spot today, I thought you might
have a wee bit of interest in the Vice Presidency and General Merchandise Managership
of Bonwit Teller's, under Mildred Custin.
Actually, Mildred is looking for a young
man who could replace her when she is
ready to retire.

Any interest?

As always, my best to you.

Sincerely,

Lillian Horinbein
President

LH/mas

G. FOX & CO. - PRESS RELEASE

For Release Monday, June 27, 1966

Ira Neimark Appointed
Vice President of G. Fox & Co.

Ira Neimark has been appointed a Vice President of G. Fox & Co., in addition to his present responsibilities as General Merchandise Manager, it was announced today by Mrs. Beatrice Fox Auerbach, President of G. Fox & Co. This appointment is part of the G. Fox & Co. continuing policy of promotion from within.

Mr. Neimark has been with G. Fox & Co. for seven years. Starting in 1959 as an assistant to the General Merchandise Manager, he soon became a Divisional Merchandise Manager. From 1961 to 1764 he was President of Brown Thomson. Shortly after returning to G. Fox & Co. he became General Merchandise Manager.

Mr. Neimark attended Columbia University School of Business and served with the 20th Air Force in the Pacific during World War II.

The new vice president is married to the former Jacqueline Myers of Providence. He has two daughters and lives in West Hartford.

Photo attached

Contact:
Paul Leblang, Advertising Director
249-9711 - Ext. 577

THE MAY DEPARTMENT STORES COMPANY

222 SOUTH MAIN STREET

AKRON 8, OHIO

July 12, 1966

Mr. Ira Neimark,
Hartford.

Dear Ira:

Thank you for your letter. I, too, will miss my contact
with you and your organization in G. Fox. They have been
most interesting so far, and one could look forward to quite
a period of development of mutual activities. This, I am
sure I shall miss throughout the company, but I have no
regrets for my decision, which as you know was a year over-
due. If it had not been for the G. Fox and Meier & Frank
acquisitions last year, I would have done this on my 60th
birthday a year ago this month.

I certainly hope that you will continue the progress you are
making in G. Fox, and that your career with May will be long
and rewarding.

Best wishes to you and your wife.

Sincerely yours,

Lincoln Gries.

LG:LK

*This letter from Lincoln Gries was the only civil communication
That I had during my association with May Department Stores*

B. ALTMAN & CO.
361 FIFTH AVENUE
NEW YORK, N.Y. 10016

MAY 13th
19 69

MAY 15

Mr. Ira Neimark
G. Fox & Co.
Hartford, Conn. 06115

Dear Ira:

Thank you for your letter of congratulations. It has been extremely
gratifying to hear from friends and
associates at this time, and I am
most grateful for your kind wishes.

Sincerely,

Randy

Randolph U. Stambaugh

*This letter from Randy Stambaugh was sent to me in reply to my
letter, congratulating him on becoming president of B. Altman & Co.
Little did I know that a month later Randy would call me to take
his place, to be the general merchandise manager at B.Altman&Co*

B Altman & Co

over the counter

AUGUST 1969

IRA NEIMARK APPOINTED VICE PRESIDENT AND GENERAL MERCHANDISE MANAGER

OPERATION SHOP EARLY – VIETNAM – 1969

In cooperation with the Red Cross, the New York store employees again have a chance to send Christmas gifts to our servicemen in Vietnam. The Red Cross has sent Ditty Bags and has suggested that they be filled with items that are needed and useful in Vietnam.

The bags may be filled by an individual or by a group, and they will be identified as gifts from Altman employees.

Each Floor has been assigned a Captain, supplied with Ditty Bags, who will approach employees as to whether they wish to participate. The completed bags must be returned to the Captains by August 27th.

In order to comply with shipping regulations, a flyer suggesting appropriate gifts has been distributed on each floor bulletin board, and at the news centers on the ninth and twelfth floors, and in the basement.

EMPLOYEE BENEFIT NOTICE

ALTMAN'S AID TO HIGHER EDUCATION

Interested in taking a course that will advance you in the knowledge of your job? If you have been on the regular payroll for at least one year, you may receive cash benefits under our Aid to Higher Education Program. Altman's will reward you with a 50% refund of the tuition cost, if the course relates indirectly to your job. If a course is directly related to your job, Altman's will refund $25.00, or 75% of the tuition cost, whichever is higher.

If you are interested in applying for this benefit, discuss it first with your Department Head or Supervisor; then see Miss Robsky in the New York Store, or the Personnel Manager in the branches.

Ira Neimark joined Altman's August 1 as Vice President and General Merchandise Manager.

Replacing Randolph Stambaugh, who was elected President April 28th, Mr. Neimark came to Altman's from G. Fox and Co., of Hartford, Conn., where he was Vice-President and General Merchandise Manager.

He is a Native New Yorker, attended Columbia University, and began his merchandising career at Bonwit Teller.

Married to the former Jaqueline Myers, of Providence, R.I., the Neimarks have two daughters, Janie and Robin.

Mr. Neimark served with the United States Army Air Force during World War II.

PARTY AT THE PLAZA

B. Altman & Co. will have a party at the Plaza Hotel on Tuesday, September 30th. At that time all employees with twenty-five or more years of service will be invited to attend a reception at The Terrace Room from 6 to 6:45 p.m., and a dinner following in The Grand Ballroom from 7 to 9 p.m.

Honor guests will be Miss Bessie Van Der Beek, of Adjustments, who is in her 70th year of employment, Miss Mary Fitzpatrick, Personnel A, and Lesley Davis, of the Bath Shop, both of whom are celebrating their 60th anniversary this year.

FASHIONS AND HANDICRAFTS FROM ISRAEL

The unique craftsmanship discovered in Israel by our own Altman representatives resulted in a month-long celebration featuring many of the native articles. To launch the promotion, a press party and fashion show was held at the Fifth Avenue Store on July 8th, honoring His Excellency Yitzhak Rabin, the Ambassador of Israel to the United States.

The play of imagination and creativity resulted in clothing for men and women that reflected the mood of the country. The natural beauty of leather and suede, woolen knits with suede and brass trimmings, original batik prints, and clean designs generated a feeling of strength and beauty – so essential to the individual image of today's fashion look.

Accessories for women were located in a special Israeli Boutique located on the Main Floor. Here one could choose from a collection of hand-woven scarves and belts; handbags; and intricate Yemenite jewelry. Colorful semi-precious stones from Edat were found in an extensive collection of rings.

Many food products were imported by Altman's and were on sale in the Delicacies area. Such exciting items included orange and lemon squash by Jaffa, Carmel grape juice in three different flavors – "muscatel," "rose," and "claret," and a tasty treat called Fatlafel, which is made by grinding chick peas, rolling them into little balls, frying, and serving them with Tehina sauce.

Handicraft is a significant and expressive form of Israeli talent. The fourth floor devoted an entire shop to the artisans. Twisted iron sculptures by David Palumbo provided dramatic decorative accents, as did the hand-thrown pottery and the hand-spun molten glassware which was moulded into geometric, floral, and figurative designs.

Decorative representations of young Israeli thought was exemplified in posters, which were screen-processed, hand-prints by E. Weishoff. Many of these posters were indicative of contemporary treatment of ancient and traditional ideas and themes.

Of special significance was a collection of pewter-washed copper. This group included tea kettles, coffee sets, decorative bowls, and attractive wall hangings.

In contrast to the contemporary approach, there were actual reproductions of beautiful old maps and antiques.

Notice of my being appointed Vice president and General merchandise manager of B. Altman & Co.

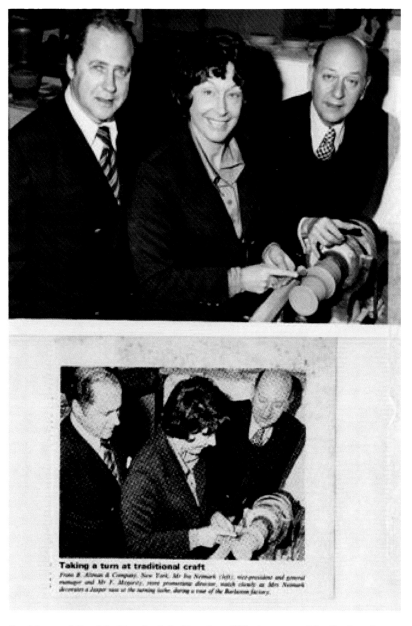

Taking a turn at traditional craft

From B. Altman & Company, New York, Mr Ira Neimark (left), vice-president and general manager and Mr F. Megarity, store promotions director, watch closely as Mrs Neimark decorates a Jasper vase at the turning lathe, during a tour of the Barlaston factory.

Jackie and I with Ferris McGarrity, Wedgewood in Ireland

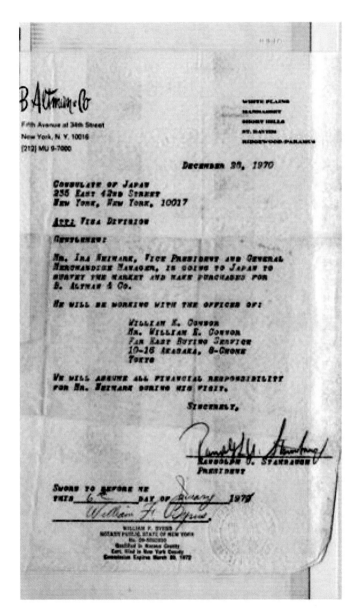

Letter from Randy Stambaugh to the Consulate of Japan for my first visit.

Marie Paris of Este and Anthony Mare of Marie designed dresses their wives wore to party. The Forum flanks the Muses.

Conservative Store Lets Its Hair Down

By BERNADINE MORRIS

Cosmetics rivals, Estée Lauder with husband, Joseph, below left, and Charles Revson and his wife, Lynn, managed not to meet at store party.

Director

Above right: Estee Lauder and Charles Revson

The announcement in *Women's Wear Daily*, Wednesday, January 29, 1975 of my being made the CEO of Bergdorf Goodman

Changing of the guard at Bergdorf Goodman: Andrew Goodman, Leonard Hankin, Neal Fox, and Ira Neimark.

Neimark to succeed Goodman as president of Bergdorf

Continued From Page One

merchandise manager of Neiman-Marcus, Dallas, will become executive vice-president and general merchandise manager, succeeding Gordon Franklin.

Franklin will assume a corporate post with Carter Hawley Hale Stores, Inc., the parent company of Bergdorf's and Neiman-Marcus, where he will develop foreign markets for the CHH department and specialty store divisions. He will headquarter in New York, but do a significant amount of traveling.

Carter Hawley Hale considers import buying a key area and does not now have a strong import program, or a liaison with import offices. CHH feels that Franklin, a former president of Saks Fifth Avenue, knows the European market and can utilize it well.

Leonard J. Hankin continues as executive vice-president of Bergdorf's. His contract with CHH has been extended until 1982, it was announced Tuesday.

Hankin and Bergdorf have each been indicted by the Justice Department's antitrust division on charges of price-fixing. Hankin has filed a motion to dismiss the charges on the grounds that he had been promised immunity and was prepared to testify, but was later denied that opportunity — the same opportunity, he said, which was granted to other retail executives.

Bergdorf's has pleaded nolo contendere to the charges and a ruling on that plea is expected next month.

Neimark, 52, is executive vice-president of B. Altman & Co. His successor there has not yet been named. He joined the six-unit Fifth Ave. department store in 1968, and was formerly with G. Fox, Hartford, Conn., as vice-president and general merchandise manager.

Goodman and Hankin, as a team, have

The ups and downs at Bergdorf Goodman

NEW YORK — Bergdorf Goodman people are wondering if last Friday's incident of a recalcitrant elevator didn't speed up management discussions between Carter Hawley Hale and Bergdorf Goodman.

It seems that Philip M. Hawley, president of CHH, and Andrew Goodman, B-G president, entered Goodman's tiny private elevator en route to the Goodman penthouse. And that's where they stayed for an hour while store personnel frantically sought a repairman.

been running the organization for many years. CHH acquired Bergdorf's when the store was doing a volume of just over $32 million. Its current volume, according to Hankin, is "around $40 million" at the main store.

Goodman and Hankin think alike and some say the top level executive staff at BG was "inbred" and new blood apparently needed.

As Goodman said Tuesday, "We are not professionals in running a five or six unit organization and the new team will have a long range program in the growth of the company."

Bergdorf still has plans for adding four units the next 10 years. Its plans for a Boston store have been sidetracked by local political problems, but it does have plans for branches in Long Island and New Jersey. Exact loca-

tions were not revealed.

Neimark and Fox, according to Goodman, are ideally suited to handle expansion plans.

Goodman admitted that the store's first branch in White Plains opened "with two strikes against it." The delay because of construction problems and the wrong timing had been costly.

He said the branch, while doing well, was running behind the $15 million volume projected for its first year. "Perhaps we were too ambitious," he said.

He also said Bergdorf's sales for January were off about 1 percent. Inventory, after selling off to Filene's basement, is now in good shape, he said.

Fox is a native New Yorker, as are Neimark, Hankin and Goodman. A graduate of City College, as is Hankin, Fox started his retail career in Brooks Bros. and Bloomingdale's while still a student. He later spent 10 years with Brooks before joining Neiman's in 1966 as men's vice-president. He became senior vice-president and general merchandise manager in December, 1972. Last year he turned down an offer to be president of Brooks Bros.

Although it is not unusual to have two executive vice-presidents in one organization, and perhaps not even unusual for BG to have four top executives with heavy merchandise backgrounds, it is apparent that the Neimark-Fox team will run the store, with the guidance of Goodman and Hankin. Hankin is expected to function much as a store manager.

Goodman, who will be 68 on Feb. 13, said he is not thinking about retirement: "I hope to continue as long as I feel I can make a contribution to Bergdorf's." He signed a five-year contract with CHH in 1972, when the Los Angeles-based company acquired Bergdorf's.

The Bergdorf Times

JUNE 1975

B.G. TWO NEW EXECUTIVES

Those two handsome men you've been seeing in and around the store since the beginning of March are Ira Neimark, our new President, and Neal J. Fox, our new Executive Vice-President and General Merchandise Manager. The B.G. Times extends a belated, but very warm welcome to them. Both of these gentlemen are "old hands" at the retailing business and bring great experience and knowledge with them to Bergdorf's.

Known in the retailing world as a "solid, down-to-earth merchandiser and a cracker-jack with figures" (WWD 2/12/75), Ira Neimark certainly comes to B.G. with excellent recommendations and Bergdorf's is proud to have a man of his superior capabilities.

A native New Yorker, Mr. Neimark attended Columbia University and began his retailing career across the street at Bonwit Teller as Blouse Buyer — he was also Assistant to the President there. In the fashion

(Continued on Page 3, Col. 1)

Born and raised in New York City, Neal J. Fox attended City College of New York and New York University Graduate School of Retailing and this year he graduates from Harvard Business School's Advanced Management Program. Mr. Fox began his career at Bloomingdale's with their "coop" training program and then spent ten years with that bastion of men's wear, Brooks Brothers. In 1966, Mr. Fox joined Neiman-Marcus in Texas as a Vice-President and Group Merchandise Director. When he left Neiman's to join B.G. he was a Senior

(Continued on Page 2, Col. 2)

Mr. Neimark

Mr. Fox

The New York Times/Jack Manning

At Bergdorf Goodman news conference, from left: Andrew Goodman, chairman; Leonard J. Hankin, executive vice president; Neal J. Fox, another executive vice president, and Ira Neimark, the company's new president.

Bergdorf Planning 4 to 6 More Stores

Bergdorf Goodman, which only three months ago opened the first suburban store in its history in White Plains, has plans for four to six more stores and is augmenting its management team for this purpose.

This was disclosed yesterday at a news conference by Andrew Goodman, president of Bergdorf, who is becoming chairman in a new management realignment. He said that new stores were being planned for Boston, New Jersey and Long Island. At least one more store is also in early planning stages in a program that Bergdorf's parent concern, Carter Hawley Hale Stores, Inc., Los Angeles, has indicated may take a decade to complete.

Ira Neimark, executive vice president of B. Altman & Co., has been named president and chief executive officer of Bergdorf and Neal J. Fox, senior vice president and general merchandise manager of Neiman-Marcus, has been appointed executive vice president and general merchandise manager of Bergdorf. Neiman-Marcus is also operated by Carter Hawley Hale.

Leonard J. Hankin continues as executive vice president of Bergdorf.

Mr. Neimark, who is 52 years old, assumes his new post at Bergdorf March 3. He, Mr. Fox and Mr. Hankin were present at the news conference held yesterday morning by Mr. Goodman at the Bergdorf store in Manhattan.

uch been running Bergdorf," r. Goodman said, "but I ink we are limited in our rizons to running a one-ore operation. I don't consider either of us professional anagers in the sense of running a 6-to 8-store operation. I think we needed some w blood, but it will take me time before both of these w men can absorb all we ."

Mr. Fox, who is 43 years old, cceeds Gordon Franklin, who ill assume corporate staff responsibility to develop foreign arkets for Carter Hawley's rious divisions.

Mr. Neimark, replying to a estion as to why he was aving Altman after five years join Bergdorf, replied "Bergof Goodman has always been

my ideal. The growth of the company should be very good."

While Mr. Goodman stressed the new appointments as being based on an expansion of the concern, trade sources indicated yesterday that Carter Hawley was moving at both Bergdorf and Neiman-Marcus to bring younger men to prepare for the eventual retirement of top executives. Mr. Goodman is 68 years old. Stanley Marcus, chairman of Neiman-Marcus, is 70 years old.

The White Plains store, which was delayed several months in its opening because of construction problems, "is doing satisfactorily and we are very bullish," Mr. Goodman said.

GUESTS

New York Life Insurance Company	Richard Kernan
Oppenheimer Management Corporation	Robert Groden
The Prudential Insurance Company of America	George Driscoll
Schroder, Naess & Thomas	Vincent Della Volpe
Union Capital Management Corp.	Robert B. Gimbel
Union Service Corp.	Ronald Mischner
U. S. Steel and Carnegie Pension Fund	Henry Thompson
United States Trust Company of N.Y.	Robert Kulig
	Charles Tlucek
Value Line Fund, Inc.	Frank Giove
E. M. Warburg, Pincus & Co. Inc.	Sheila Scott

Carter Hawley Hale Stores, Inc.

EDWARD W. CARTER, *Chairman of the Board*

PHILIP M. HAWLEY, *President*

HOWARD N. WEST, *Vice President and Treasurer*

IRA NEIMARK, *President and Chief Executive Officer of Bergdorf Goodman*

Morgan Stanley & Co. Incorporated

DONALD H. MCALLISTER, *Managing Director*

JOHN H. T. WILSON, *Managing Director*

JOSEPH M. SELF, *Vice President*

STEPHEN C. WHITMAN

JOSEPH A. ZOLLO

MORRIS E. ZUKERMAN

6/9/75

The graphs show after three years of bringing top fashion houses to Bergdorf, sales increased dramatically. Profits increased dramatically as well, due to the management of inventories using the units weeks of supply procedure.

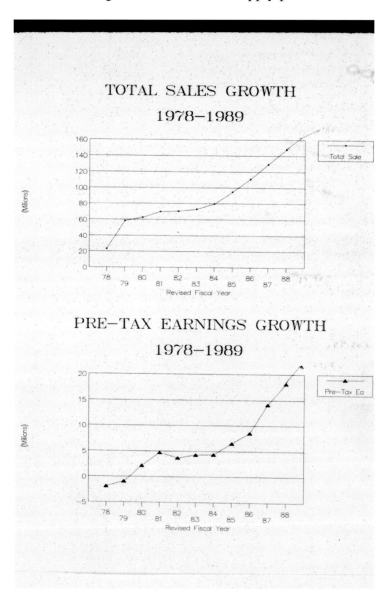

Getting Personal

Now on to my enjoyable priorities of a lifetime, that helped me make the enjoyable transition from a successful business career to a Successful, Happy and Healthy Retirement,

Golf
My Reading Habit
Writing a Memoir of My Life for Young Family Members
Involvement with Business and Educational Organizations
Stepping into the Electronic Age
Dining In
Dining Out
Travel
Flying/Sailing
My Cameras
Stamp and Coin Collecting
Entertainment
Exercise
Smoking
Liberal Arts
Keeping Up to Date
Driving
Doctors, Medicine and Good Health
Sleep
Beer, Wine and Whiskey
Relationships
Social Relationships
Business Relationships
Summary

Golf

I have found that having an enjoyable and healthy sport in retirement has many benefits beyond that of keeping busy. The one sport that has answered my requirements is golf. Golf has always offered me fresh air, exercise, challenges and ever-lasting friendships.

Again I am reminded of two examples to make this point.

A number of years ago I met a very successful retailer who had retired. He complained to me that he made a mistake when he gave up golf for sailing. His reason, sailing is in many cases a solo experience, whereas when he played golf he had many golf friends. Now that he has given up sailing, at this late age, he has no friends to play golf with. That doesn't mean sailing is not a good sport. More about that later on.

Here is the other example: I have noticed that a number of the senior golfers I play with are former tennis players. In each and every case they explain that playing tennis has, over the years, damaged their knees, making golf, at their current age, their chosen sport. Fortunately or not, I never played tennis. This is not to say there was no other sport for me to enjoy.

I have fished for salmon in Canada and bass in my pond, enjoyed deep-sea fishing and bone fishing in the Bahamas, and so on. Bowling throughout my youth, hiking on the Appalachian Trail, sailing on Long Island Sound, etc., etc.—they all have something to make my retirement life enjoyable. But golf, in many ways for me, encompasses something that all of these and other sports have in common.

In addition to all the outdoor activities listed above, a very fortunate incident happened in 1970, when we moved into our new home in Harrison, New York.

I hired a bulldozer to clear out a lot of roughage, dead trees, old vines and such in a large area behind our house. In the process, the bulldozer uncovered a farmer's drain with running water. I then directed the bulldozer operator to dig an area approximately ten thousand square feet, five feet deep, to form a pond similar to those ponds that I saw in English country magazines.

Over these many years, I have stocked the pond with largemouth bass. I fished for the bass, and of course, threw them back. More recently, I just enjoy seeing them swim around in what is essentially my own aquarium.

I have also found hitting golf balls over the pond into the woods behind the house an enjoyable exercise, as well as excellent practice.

A photo taken while I was hiking and camping in Bear Mountain State Park is included in the insert. A boy scout friend of mine and I would take the subway to 181st Street, walk across the George Washington Bridge, then thumb a hitching ride to Bear mountain. In those days, it was normal for young people to hitchhike, without too much trouble. Sorry to say, this seems to be no longer possible.

I first became interested in golf when I was about twelve years old. I bought a driver in a pawnshop. I was able to find golf balls behind a driving range near Floyd Bennett Airfield. I began swinging at golf balls in the sand in what is now Jamaica Bay Wild Life Refuge. Starting to play golf with no lessons is equivalent to picking up a violin and hoping to play Mozart. It just doesn't work.

Like anything else, I had to be guided by professionals.

Over the years, when I was active in business, as well as retired, I have been fortunate to play golf not only at golf clubs I belonged to in Providence, Rhode Island; West Hartford, Connecticut; Purchase, New York; and fortunately some of the best in the world.

My most memorable golf event happened when, in London in 1987, I attended a reception for Princess Diana.

My wife and I had been introduced to Princess Diana at a previous reception, as well as my being her dinner partner at an event honoring English fashion designers. At this reception one of her equerries, knowing I had my golf clubs with me on this trip, recommended that I ask the princess if I might play golf at Windsor. When my turn came to be greeted by the princess, after small chatter reminding her of my wearing her favorite Turnbull & Asser blue necktie, (which she said, matched my eyes) I asked, would it be possible for me to play golf at Windsor Castle? Princess Diana looked at her equerry and me and said, "You boys are always looking for trouble."

When I got back to my hotel there was a message from Windsor Castle. Would I please be ready at 9:00 a.m. the next morning? A car would pick me up with my clubs and take me to Windsor Castle. Naturally, I wore my blazer and grey flan - nels, prepared to change into my golf clothes at the castle. That was not to be. Instead there was a small caddy shack where golfers changed into golf clothes.

I noticed that the golf course had an awful lot of divots. I was told the divots were from the royals riding their horses on the golf course.

The sand traps also looked messed up. Again the answer was that the royal children played in the sand traps with their pails and shovels.

I was also told that whenever members of the royal family are at Windsor, guest are not invited to play golf. Princess Diana took care of that problem by saying, "Mr. Neimark will be playing golf today with members of my staff, tend to it."

Needless to say, of all the golf courses where I have played and will play, golf at Windsor Castle as a guest of Princes Diana was an unforgettable event. The photo documentation of my Windsor round is on the cover of this book.

Another memorable event was playing at The New Delhi Golf Club in India in 1973 when I was visiting Mrs. Sahni, B. Altman's commissioner in India. She invited me to play golf at her golf club.

It seems that, at one point in history, there was possibly a very old Indian cemetery where the golf club stands today. At each tee was a monument of some sort. I was told the British converted the area to a golf course in the nineteenth century.

We not only had a foursome and two caddies, but, as golf balls were prohibitively expensive, we also had two ball boys to find the golf balls before the monkeys all over the golf course did. Needless to say, more than a few golf balls were lost to the monkeys.

In my travels I was very fortunate to play golf in some of the most wonderful and famous courses in countries around the world: The United States, Scotland, Ireland, England, Italy, France, Japan, Portugal, Morocco and India.

Golf games in some countries had peculiar customs. In Morocco, the concierge at my hotel told me my golf game was moved to the afternoon since the king of Morocco was playing in the morning and the Marrakesh Golf Course was closed. I won't go onto the idiosyncrasies of golf in different countries, other than to say, every game was a wonderful experience.

A number of years ago when I played golf at Saint Andrews in Scotland, I noticed in the clubhouse, a large, imposing frame with the following declaration, which I have never forgotten:

GOLF

Golf is a science, the study of a lifetime, in which you may exhaust yourself never your subject. It is a contest, a duel, or a melee calling for courage, energy and self-control. It is a test of temper, a trial of honour, revealer of character. It affords a chance to play the man and act the gentleman. It means going into God's out-of-doors, getting close to nature, fresh air, exercise, a sweeping away of mental cobwebs, genuine recreation of tired tissues. It includes close relationships with friends, social intercourse, opportunities for courtesy, kindness and generosity to an opponent. It promotes not only physical health but moral force.

That says it all.

My Reading Habit

All my life ever since I first learned to read, books have been one of my most enjoyable activities.

Early on, when I was about eight or nine years old, I rented Tom Swift, Don Sturdy and Jack Armstrong action books for young readers for ten cents from a small bookstore near where I lived. Since then I have had the pleasure of reading hundreds of books that are in my overflowing library.

One of my early memories of collecting books started with a newspaper, *The New York Telegram*. By collecting a certain number of coupons from the newspaper, plus 25 cents you could select a limited number of books. My first purchase was in 1936. I bought four beautifully bound books by Mark Twain, plus a two volume *Webster's Dictionary*. I still have the Mark Twain books to remind of when I started my collection.

Before retiring, I found reading while traveling covered a lot of ground. Reading at bedtime and into the night also added to my reading time.

Now that I have been retired these many-years, I find setting a reading schedule for an hour or so after my nap, in the afternoon also covers a lot of ground.

Another most enjoyable habit is to read *The New York Times Book Review* section from cover to cover each week.

I also remember how amazed I was, at about twelve years old, to discover the wonderful Public Library on Martense Street in Brooklyn. Walking into that imposing building was like walking into a candy store. I never knew where to begin.

After a while I concentrated on biographies. Reading as many biographies as I could of people who achieved great success seemed to give me the impetus to be successful in the many challenges that faced me.

Now in the amazing age of electronics, I find ordering many books instantly—biographies, history, art, etc.—from Amazon on my Kindle is truly magical compared to my early reading days.

Writing a Memoir of My Life for Young Family Members

Somewhere around ten years after I retired from Bergdorf Goodman, I gave up advisory positions with different companies due to the annoyance of air travel and schedules that interfered with my leisure time. At that time, my granddaughters Hallie Seegal and Pam Lewis, asked why was the number 721 so important to me? I told them that was my lucky number; I always used it for car license plates, etc. as a reminder of the beginning of my fortunate business career.

When I learned how to type on my computer by using "Mario Teaches Typing," I was off and running.

Initially I wrote a letter to my granddaughters explaining 721 was the address of Bonwit Teller, 721 Fifth Avenue, where I started my retail career at Christmas time in 1938. I found it rewarding to relate to my grandchildren how fortunate I was to be hired by Bonwit Teller, one of the leading fashion stores in New York, to be a pageboy in their 721 Club. Also, how important it was for me to be recognized by key executives. I particularly impressed the president of the store on my first day on the job, by greeting him (he had been pointed out by the floor walker) with, "Good morning Mr. Holmes." Mr. William M. (Bill) Holmes then became my mentor—when I was a mere sixteen going on seventeen years of age. Mr. Holmes later told me how impressed he was that, on my first day on the job, I not only knew his name but also had the good manners to say good morning. He also directed the personnel department to hold on to this boy after Christmas. "He has a future here."

I enjoyed writing that long letter to my granddaughters so much that I continued writing until I completed my first book, *Crossing Fifth Avenue to Bergdorf Goodman*. That book kept me busy with speaking engagements at business schools such as Columbia, New York University and The Wharton School. Other business forums followed until I decided they were taking up too much of my retirement time.

An interesting aside: Being a high school dropout during The Great Depression always bothered me, as I did not have the formal educational requirements necessary in the business world.

The business education that I received at Bonwit Teller more than made up for any lack of not attending business school. However, after I returned home from WWII in 1946, Erasmus Hall high school awarded me a graduation diploma. This, by their logic, was based on my passing all the tests necessary to become an Aviation Cadet.

In addition, Bonwit Teller granted me a scholarship to Columbia University night classes. I attended these classes in 1941, 1942, and again after the war, beginning in 1946.

I was appointed adjunct professor at the Business School during the 1983 and 1984 terms. Following that, I was guest lecturer at the Business School for the next five years. Based on the above, Columbia granted me the title of Alumnus.

Again, I accomplished another of my goals.

When I mentioned writing my stories for my grandchildren to my retired and soon to be retired business and social friends, their response was, in many cases, that they didn't use computers. My advice; Get a yellow pad and start writing. Your children and their children will always thank you for it.

As you can see, I am still writing and enjoying every minute of it.

Involvement with Business and Educational Organizations

Many successful businessmen, as well as other professionals, have found their many years of experience have value for newly evolving and long established companies. Some companies, like Hermès of Paris, asked me to be a board member. Mitsukoshi, in Japan, retained me as an advisor, as did the House of Frazer in London and a few others.

Serving on various boards and as an advisor to companies as varied as those in the United States, France, England, Italy, Japan and India during my early years of retirement was like a second career. However, as the years went by, some of

these positions required more time and travel than seemed fit -
ting for my priorities. Having my own time at some point had
more value for me than having to be available for other people's schedules.

One of most rewarding of all these activities was lecturing at Columbia Business School. Professor Mark Cohen invited me to be a guest lecturer in his class on Leadership. I have
found undergraduates and MBAs to be enormously interested
in learning what it takes and how to achieve successful business careers. There is great satisfaction in hearing from students over the years who thank me for giving them some of the
keys to open their doors to success. The interest of the students
in these lectures led me to write more about my experiences in
the retail and business world that might benefit them.

When I had my first book published, I had the good for
tune to meet two very generous supporters interested in my
telling the story of how I found a gold mine on Fifth Avenue.

One was Gregory Furman. Greg is the founder and
CEO of the Luxury Marketing Council. He had the brilliant
idea of having the leading luxury companies join his Council to exchange information about how they developed their
businesses' successes, and ideas for achieving further growth.
He initially started with luxury companies like Neiman Marcus, Bergdorf Goodman, Cartier, etc. I believe that today The
Luxury Marketing Council has thousands of luxury members
around the world.

Greg started me on speaking tours to members of his
Marketing Council, which, much to my surprise, I enjoyed, and
hopefully the audiences did as well. I will be eternally grateful
to Greg.

At that time, I also met Robert Reiss. Robert came from
another direction, but in my opinion, with same brilliant mar-

keting idea. Starting with the CEO radio show, a media platform to communicate thoughts and ideas to other CEOs, he now publishes *The CEO Forum*, by CEOs and for CEOs. He graciously included my story in one of his issues.

All three men, Professor Mark Cohen, Greg Furman, and Robert Reiss, were generous with their time and experience, helping me realize I had a story to tell, and how to tell it.

These books, *Crossing Fifth Avenue to Bergdorf Goodman, The Rise of Fashion and Lessons Learned at Bergdorf Goodman*, *A Retailer's Lifetime of Lessons Learned*, and *The Rise of Bergdorf Goodman and the Fall of Bonwit Teller* brought about a good number of book sales from students attending my lectures. This proved to me that young people today are as interested in learning from experienced executives as students were in my day.

One disappointment, though, occurred in 1983. When I was CEO of Bergdorg Goodman, I was invited to be an adjunct professor at Columbia Business School. I held the position for two terms. I found the experience interesting until I volunteered to introduce my class to any retail CEO they would like to meet, to further their careers. Not one of the 39 students took me up on my offer.

It showed me that undergraduates and MBAs were not aware the importance of networking; plus, they all wanted to work on Wall Street. They were not aware that retail CEOs were working with Wall Street to finance their expansions.

I learned early on—watching executives when I was eighteen years old and the office boy to the president of Bonwit Teller— that networking was one of the keys to success.

Years later, lecturing at Columbia brought me a wonderful feeling of nostalgia: In 1940, I was the office boy   to the president and the scholarship from Bonwit's Royalty Fund enabled me to attend night classes at Columbia. There I was, nineteen years old, picking up where I left off as a high school dropout, when I left Erasmus Hall to go to work.

The wonderful campus and the historic buildings, the environment, and my classes then showed me that there were greater opportunities out there, and gave me the boost and impetus to achieve them.

Stepping into the Electronic Age

I will always recall, when I was about seven or eight years of age, what my father said to me: "One day there will be a magic box, that when you press a button, will answer any question that you will have." That magical comment of his stayed in my mind all these many years.

Naturally, my father had no idea how right he was. Fortunately, I lived to see the miracle of the electronic age. "The magic box" arrived in the form of my computer.

Since my handwriting is unintelligible, making it difficult for me to write letters and other requirements for writ - ten communication, I found the computer to be the answer to my prayers. I was able to write reasonable letters, and as mentioned, lectures and books. With Spell Check, a dictionary and a thesaurus at my fingertips, I was liberated.

Since I retired, I have had the time available to slowly, very slowly, learn the many opportunities and conveniences that come with the use of my computer. The magic box allows me to communicate not only with my present generation, but also my children and their children.

Being able to communicate with, and send photographs and birthday, holiday and anniversary greetings to three generations of my family is an achievement that I really enjoy.

In addition, I have found that for writing books, or preparing for lectures at business schools, my computer is invaluable, enabling me to find names and places, facts and figures.

For my generation, before the computer, researching and finding required information for books or lectures was a formidable task. Any number of books were required—from my own collection or local and distant libraries—which would take hours, and sometime days, to research. Now, with a click or two, the information that I am looking for appears instantly on my computer.

I could only wish that my father could see what he had the imagination and brilliance to forecast, back in the 1920s. What has happened electronically since then is far beyond his and my wildest dreams.

Dining In

All throughout my business career, I enjoyed having dinner at home with my wife and children. My commute home, from the city, was relatively short. When I arrived home, I left my briefcase at the door, not to be opened until the next day.

Retelling my business adventures of the day to my wife and my two daughters, Janie and Robin, was most entertaining and enjoyable, as always was the dinner. Continuing the habit of dining at home, with Jackie, in a relaxed environment has, I am sure, contributed to the enjoyment of my retirement.

I often think back to the time when I was attending night school classes at Erasmus Hall. After delivering laundry and groceries, then having dinner with my mother and brothers, it was a challenge, after dinner, to pick up and attend classes until late in the evening.

Later, when I attended Columbia night classes after work at Bonwit Teller, getting on the Fifth Avenue bus to class es was easy. I had a quick sandwich, at Chock Full o' Nuts, and went across Broadway directly to my classes.

Dining Out

Fortunately, when I arrived back in New York City, from New England in 1970, I was reintroduced to some famous restaurants that I had frequented years earlier, such as 21. However, once joining Bergdorf Goodman, I had the opportunity, both in the United States and Europe, to visit all the best restaurants in the world.

I won't go on to mention them other to than to say, that each in its own way left me with an indelible impression of its excellence, great service and enjoyable dining.

Naturally, in retirement, the opportunities to dine at so many excellent locations grew more limited. I found that the convenience and enjoyment of fine dining was best preserved by choosing a few, very select, restaurants—preferably local.

Local would also include New York City. However, my preference is above 42nd Street: 21, Doubles, and Cipriani. Locally: my golf club, Century has excellent dining, as do La Panetière, and Gus's. La Panetière is a wonderful French restaurant that reminds my wife and me of the restaurants where we dined when we traveled through France. Gus's is like an Irish pub. All three are within easy driving distance. The reasons we like them: The few restaurants that my wife and I frequent, know that we are "regulars." Usually there is no problem with a reservation, a favorite table, and the owner and staff seeing to it that we are treated as valued, steady customers (the best kind). This contrasts with "a great new restaurant" recommended by friends. It may be great, but unfortunately it is often disadvantaged by the maître d' or the captain walking me so far back, that I usually say, "any further back will give me a nose bleed." Not being a steady is like being a stranger in a strange land.

As I get older, convenience and proper service become necessary requirements.

In 1947, one of my first experiences dining out was being invited to lunch for the very first time at 21. The secretary to the president of Bonwit Teller, Betty Vanderbilt, called to ask me if I wore my hat to work that day? I did. She said Mr. Rudolph, Bonwit Teller's new president, would like to take you to lunch, at 21. Wearing your hat, in those days, was required to show that you knew how to dress properly.

Needless to say, I was very impressed. I was also told, at that lunch, that I was being promoted to assistant to the president.

Since then, my wife and I have dined there many times. This includes a special dinner party, in honor of Giorgio Armani opening his shop, at Bergdorf Goodman.

Travel

My first overseas trip, to Europe, in 1967, was recom - mended by Beatrice Fox Auerbach, president and owner of G.Fox & Co., Hartford, Connecticut. At that time, I had been promoted to vice president, general merchandise manager. In that position, I was entitled to certain perks: traveling first class, staying at the hotels of my choice, as well as my wife accompanying me on these business trips. Jackie did, when it was convenient to have her mother stay with our two young children.

It would seem BFA, as she was called (without her knowledge), had interest in my continuing, with her taste level, in leading the stores merchants. With that in mind, she recommended that I stay at hotels where, over the years, she and her family had stayed on their many trips to Europe. Among them: The Ritz Hotel, in Paris, The Hassler, in Rome, and The Connaught, in London.

Needless to say, all three were the height of luxury. As it turned out, my first trip to those hotels was an eye opener. The luxury, elegance and service, plus the famous landmarks in each of the famous cities, left me with indelible impressions of what BFA had intended.

I recall calling Jackie, from my first stop, the Hassler, in Rome, saying, "I arrived safely and you will have to make the next trip." Which she did.

On the next trip Jackie was able to accompany me. She too was overwhelmed with famous cities and their landmarks, which she had heard about since she was very young.

The most memorable moment was when we arrived at The Ritz, in Paris. Jackie had tears of joy. "It is all so beautiful!"

Fortunately, these trips were continued for the next twenty-five years (as I moved from G. Fox, to B. Altman and finally to Bergdorf Goodman); so much so, that we became regulars at the Ritz, always having the junior suite we preferred.

The extra memorable moments came when the Concord was our means of travel—starting in 1977 and lasting throughout almost 50 flights of our comings and goings to Paris and London—for most of the time I was CEO of Bergdorf Goodman. The many trips were required to attend the European couture shows, held twice a year in January and July, and the ready to wear shows, also twice a year in spring and fall.

Additionally, we had the use of a chauffeuring service. In France, the driver, Domonique, was an excellent tour director. On weekends, he would drive us to the most beautiful palaces, in France, furthering BFA's wish for me to acquire her taste level. We also visited many of the famous wine cellars, as well as French country restaurants, just outside of Paris.

In Paris, meetings began with breakfasts at the Ritz with our merchandise executives, then lunches with fashion houses, and, finally, dinners at our favorite restaurants—including, at that time, L'Orangerie.

It is easy to see: Developing Bergdorf Goodman to be the leading fashion retailer, being able to live in the height of luxury over the many years, and, ultimately, retiring to a comfortable and enjoyable life style, was very important. When I arrived at that stage of my life, after years of travel, stress, anxiety and pressure—all that goes with building a successful business career—being able to relax and enjoy peace and quiet became the required goal.

Unfortunately today, at this stage of my life, I have found that travel should be avoided wherever and whenever possible.

There was a time, as written about above, when travel was a luxury. During the 50s and 60s, traveling was a special experience. Passengers on both planes and trains dressed for the occasion. In the early 70s, when the Boeing Jumbo Jet 747 became the plane of choice for long distances, luxury travel became the norm for much larger audiences.

As mentioned, the greatest luxury of all was the Concord, operated jointly by Air France and British Air. The first of my many Concord flights, over a twenty-year period, was on January 27, 1977. This was on Inauguration Day for Jimmy Carter. The Concord flew out of Washington, DC, then New York's JFK a few years later.

Compared to commercial flying today, the Concord was like something out of science fiction. Let me explain. When you arrived at the airport, JFK here in the States, or Heathrow or De Gaulle, in England or France, respectively, you found that the Concord Lounge was set up for comfort and convenience. Luggage was checked and boarding passes were issued, with no long lines. Coats were checked, to be given back upon arrival. Snacks and liquor, of all types, were available. When the flight was called, there was a casual walk to the plane, with courteous greetings by attractive flight attendants; English accents on British Air, and French accents on Air France. The seating was assigned, front section to rear section, all first class. Be - fore take-off, champagne was immediately served with caviar. Trays were cleared before the plane took off. After take-off, a wonderful lunch was served. The flight from New York City to Paris that we normally booked took off at 9:00 a.m., which was mid-afternoon in Paris, After three and a half hours' flight time, at 1,350 mph—twice the speed of sound, the jet got us to our hotel at about 7: 00 p.m., just in time to change for dinner.

The reverse was the same, taking off from Paris or London. I was back at my desk, in New York at about 10 o'clock in the morning.

Those days are long gone. With high gas prices, a hundred passengers, paying a thousand dollars, is not financially practical, compared to larger planes seating hundreds more passengers and generating greater profits.

The enjoyment and luxury of air traveled changed dramatically in 1978, with the Airline Deregulation Act. This is not to say that the Deregulation Act was not a good thing. In many ways, it was. There were good and bad years for the airline industry, but it was surely a great benefit for the public. With prices and airlines competing for customers, nearly everyone who wanted to travel by air could now afford to do so.

What has this to do with my retirement? Air travel has become a very uncomfortable and unenjoyable method of travel for senior retirees like me. It interferes with my goal of a comfortable and relaxed life style.

While I traveled to and from Europe many times during the 70s, 80s and early 90s, on 747s and the Concord, in what today would be considered sheer luxury, the mere thought of taking a flight today, for the want of a better expression, really turns me off. The long and slow lines, like cattle chutes, checking in, followed by longer lines for passing through security, are annoying. Airline scheduled departure and arrival times are seldom achieved. Adding insult to injury, with so many children now flying, and with their parents thinking that children screaming is the norm, I have reached the limit of my patience. I experienced the golden age of flying.

There are airlines that still believe in and deliver luxury flights and service. They are not inexpensive. My financial planner, as I mentioned, has made these exceptions possible. As for trains, Amtrak serves its purpose, getting you to where you want to go, with a minimum of fuss.

In the 1980s, Jackie and I were invited to the Orient Express's initial run, from Venice to London. Here too was an experience in luxury travel that cannot be equaled.

Lastly, I drive to local destinations. However, I rarely drive at night. With roads and avenues clogged, on the way to and back from New York City, I find it a necessary convenience to hire off duty policemen to drive for me. This eliminates the stress and strain. Imperative for relaxation.

Many of my retired friends take cruises, as a wonderful way to relax and to see the world. Jackie and I have taken two that were memorable. One was to St. Petersburg, by way of Europe, and the other, to the Greek Islands. Both were very enjoyable. However, at our ripe old age, the fuss and bother of preparing and travel to ports, is more than we care to go through now.

Flying/Sailing

My love affair with flying began when I was six years old. Charles Lindbergh's 1927 solo, nonstop flight over the Atlantic, from New York to Paris, in 33 1/2 hours, turned me and many of the young boys of my generation into aviation enthusiasts.

When Lindbergh returned from Paris, my father took me and my older brother, Lester, to see Lindbergh's parade up Broadway. The parade attracted a few million people. So many, in fact, that we could get no closer than a block away from Broadway. Nevertheless, that was a day that left an indelible impression in my memory.

Building model airplanes kept our enthusiasm up, until some of us had the opportunity to actually fly.

My first opportunity came on a summer Sunday, at Floyd Bennett Field, when I was just ten years old. Pilots would offer rides for $5.00, for a short flight. I asked my father to buy a ticket for me to get a ride in a not too old looking biplane. He bought the ticket. However, my mother overruled him, thus eliminating my bragging rights, at school, about being the first one in my class to fly.

My first flight came when I was thirteen years old. During the summer, my older brother, Lester, and I would ride our bikes to Floyd Bennett field to take a swim in Jamaica Bay, behind the airport. One day, on our way home, I saw a young man washing down his plane, near the guard fence. My brother went home while I stood at the fence, transfixed by being so close to an airplane.

The man invited me in to help him.

After that chore, he invited me for a short flight. As the plane, an Aeronca C3, pilot and passenger, side by side, took off I could see and feel the plane rising into the blue sky. I was, figuratively speaking, in heaven.

That flight and a number of others with that pilot, Bud Frazier, led me years later to enlist, as an aviation cadet, in the Army Air Corps, in 1942.

That I passed both the mental and physical exams was a wonder to me. I took the mental exam with about 200 other volunteers, and was surprised to learn that I was one of the only fifty, or so, who passed.

Considering that I was a high school dropout, this conveyed to me the possibility that I might have what is called "native intelligence." The physical was also a surprise; even being underweight, I made it.

Being sworn in as an Air Corps reservist, until my class was ready to be called up, bothered me. Here I signed up six months after we entered the war, and I would still have to wait to be called up. Possibly the war would end before I got in.

That possibility, of course, was not to be. In February, I received my notice to report on March 3rd. My first stop was Nashville, Tennessee, for classification of pilot, bombardier or navigator.

As I wished and hoped for, I was classified for pilot training.

I don't want to go into war stories; I really have none to tell, except one. After the war ended, waiting on Saipan to come home, I was assigned to the 73rd Wing Compound, where all surplus war equipment was stored. My responsibility was to help decide what equipment was to be sent back to the U.S., and what equipment was to be left and destroyed.

One day, my team and I went looking for souvenirs. We were very lucky not to be able to get into a cave, pock marked by shells from the U.S. Marines invasion of Saipan, a year earlier.

The cave was about twenty feet above the ocean; however, the waves would wash up that high, making it difficult to enter the cave (by climbing around a cliff) without being washed into the ocean. We figured that each of us could get through to the cave, if we waited to try between the waves.

Fortunately, the first to try, Norm Mattern, was half way around the cliff when a wave came up and washed him into the ocean. Norm was not a good swimmer, and all we could see was his hat floating in the water.

The next wave came up, and he was washed up and down before we could grab him. We were ready the second time. With others holding on to my belt, on the next big wave, I was able to reach Norm's arm and pulled him to safety. We left the cliff without souvenirs. No damage, except for Norm requiring treatment for his hands being cut by the coral and rocks.

I said, "fortunately." A week later, a Japanese captain and ten of his royal marines, who were hiding out in that cave, surrendered.

I often wondered, if we had gotten into the cave, would the Japanese have surrendered to us, making us heroes, or would we have been casualties of war? The Japanese captain's formal surrender took place a week or so later, luckily without our being involved.

In a remarkable coincidence, I left for the   Air Corps on March 3, 1943, and returned home on March 3, 1946, after serving with the 20th Air Force in the Pacific theatre (with a stop off at Boca Raton as a radar instructor for a most interesting year).

On my last night at Columbia University, before leaving for the war, for good luck, I touched the toes of the statues at the entrance to the campus, on Broadway, and made the wish: I will touch the toes when I return. With a lot of good luck, I did.

What has this to do with retirement? Nothing, but memories of adventure in my younger years, and a reminder of the wonders of flight, and the enjoyment of flying.

In 1978, I bought a second hand, 28 foot Dufor sailboat. I named it True Love, for Jackie. I was able to have it docked at Tide Mill Yacht Basin, a small, very old boatyard in Rye, New York on Long Island Sound. I sailed it sometimes solo, but many times with Jackie and, sometimes, also a young skipper, for when I was lazy or wanted to take a nap.

My habit then, on weekends, was to play golf on Sunday morning, with my regular foursome, then go sailing in the afternoon. I later sold the boat when I retired, which I often think may have been a mistake.

My Cameras

I had my first camera when I was about twelve years old—a small thing, possibly made in Japan. I was mesmerized with taking the film out of the camera, putting it through three trays of chemicals, and then watching the negatives slowly develop. This to me, then, was magic. I never got over that experience.

Over the years, I have had many types of cameras—too many to mention, other than to say that I have gone from a small black and white camera to color, Polaroid, 35mm, Argus, Minox and, today, to a Nikon that uses no film and is all elec - tronic. I even, periodically, use a cell phone

Ever since I got my first one, I nearly always had a camera at various family events. So much so, that over many, many years I have amassed not hundreds, but thousands of pictures.

What has all this have to do with my retirement?

I found, that if and when I had some free time, it was most enjoyable to sort out and organize the many shoeboxes full of photos that I accumulated over those many years—from a good number that date back to before the war, to those as recent as a birthday party for my wife, Jackie.

Organizing the photos, I must say, was the hard part. The easy, and again magical, part was sending the photos to a company, in California, that put them all the on DVDs. The results are gratifying in a number of ways:

First, by ordering several DVDs, I have enough to give them as gifts to members of my family.

Second, young family members can view the DVDs on their computers. Older and non-computer using family members can view as many pictures as they want on their TVs.

Third, and the way I enjoy the most, is that I can scroll through the DVDs on my computer, find a wonderfully cute baby picture and e-mail it to the person in the picture—usually one of our children or grandchildren.

This, then, is another hobby that has given me tremendous enjoyment and pleasure, and allowed me to reflect back, in time, to what it was that Jackie and I have accomplished, over a good part of our lives.

Stamp and Coin Collecting

Like many young boys of my time, stamp and coin collecting was a very important part of learning history—not only about America, but also about the world around us.

I started collecting Indian Head pennies when my uncle Jack gave me one from the year 1859, the first year Indian Heads were minted. My coin-collecting hobby was on. After that, I had an arrangement with a lady who owned a candy store in our neighborhood. She would save the Indian heads for me for a nickel apiece. This was in 1934 when Indian Heads were plentiful.

I had reached the point of having a complete collection from 1859 through 1909, the last year they were minted. Then, when I was 12 or 13 years old, and money was very scarce, I had to make a decision that has stayed with me all these years.

My brothers and I wanted to buy a football. I reluctantly used all my Indian Heads to buy the football. Of course, the football is long gone and so was my Indian Head collection.

During my retirement, I decided to resurrect my long lost Indian Head collection and have the enjoyment of reliving the coin collection of my youth.

I have, on my desk, about twenty-five Indian Heads (as well as some Buffalo nickels) to look at and enjoy each day, including one from 1859.

From time to time I contact coin companies searching for the few years that I am still missing. My ambition is to make it up to that 14 year-old boy and return the collection he spent on a football.

I had a few stamp collections then, as well. As good as and as complete as they were, stamps never had the magic that coins had for me. Trying to imagine who owned the old coins and where they were used in the Civil War captivated my imagination.

This I could not imagine with postage stamps. There was, however, an incident with stamps that made my being a stamp collector very worthwhile.

When France surrendered to Germany in 1940, I was the office boy to the president of Bonwit Teller. One of the last boxes of dresses to leave France was sent to Bonwit Teller from their French Commissionaire in Paris. When it arrived, the box was covered with 50 Franc stamps. As I was the office boy to the president, and the staff knew that I was a stamp collector, I was given the box. I recall taking the box wrapping home and soaking the stamps, from the wrapping, in the bathtub.

I sold all of the 50 Franc stamps to a collector for $18.00. That summer I bought a canoe with the money and I paddled it in the Hudson River. When the summer ended, I sold the canoe for a grey flannel suit that would befit an office boy to the president.

Retirement, I have found, can be made more enjoyable by rectifying the small errors made in my youth.

Entertainment

When I was very young, going to the movies was an occasion. There were many movie houses in every neighborhood. This made it quite easy to see whatever movie my mother would select for our Saturday afternoon movie outing.

I mention this since, in those days, movies were silent with what we call today "closed captions." The sound came from an organ playing music determined by the mood on the screen.

This was, of course, very different from today, with many movie houses located in or near malls, and with televisions, cell phones, and other gadgets that eliminate the adventure of movie-going for many people.

The movie houses, in some cases, were miniature Radio City Musical Halls. They were built like small palaces to create a luxurious environment. There were, later on, outdoor movies, allowing people to see the movies from their autos.

Best of all, the admission prices were very inexpensive, allowing the theatres to always be filled. In the 1920s-30s, going to the movies was the most inexpensive and popular entertainment for everyone of all ages and incomes.

Jackie said her Mom would give her 10 cents, plus a penny for candy, when she went to the movies with her girl-friends.

I don't recall movies being more than 25 cents in those days. This included double features, with in-between short films.

The well to do, it seemed, went to the theatre. My family would have been considered upper middle-class, hence the movie theatre was our weekly destination. This is not to say, however, that my mother and father never went to the theatre. They talked about seeing *George White Scandals*, *Ziegfield Follies* and other Broadway shows.

Our Brooklyn neighborhood was Flatbush. Our neighbors were, in most cases, professionals: lawyers, as was my father, doctors, accountants and so on. Life was easy and enjoyable for the young and old.

Prosperity was on the rise, after WWI, allowing most families in my neighborhood to have new automobiles. In our case, my father drove a Chevrolet with a rumble seat. Many times, when he visited his clients, he would invite my brothers Lester and Bert, and me to ride in the rumble seat.

The rides that stand out in my memory are the ones when we drove to Canarsie. This was an area in Brooklyn, populated by farms operated mainly by the newest wave of Italian immigrants. In the process, my father learned to speak Italian, quite fluently. I recall his clients piling fruit and small tomatoes into the car for us to take home. Great fun!

A bit later on, my father bought my mother our famous black Marmon. She wasted no time in having the car painted lavender.

Now, back to the movies. In our neighborhood, there were a number of movie theatres: Kenmore, Albemarle, Rialto, The Patio, and a bit later on, the magnificent Lowe's Kings (which recently has been renovated into a music hall). They were all located within a mile of where we lived. We all looked forward to Saturday afternoon, when my mother, brothers and I would visit the theater showing the movie of her choice.

For a while, my aunt and my cousins joined the crowd to see the latest movie hit. A real family affair.

Silent movies prevailed, with stars such as Charlie Chaplin, Harold Lloyd, and Buster Keaton for comedy and Valentino, Norma Shearer, and Joan Crawford for romance. My mother always chose romance, allowing us once in a while to see a war movie, like *The Big Parade*, or *The Dawn Patrol*. That movie was at the Kenmore, where they had the fuselage of a WWI fighter plane in the lobby. I was hooked, at that point, on being a pilot.

Then, in 1927, I remember seeing and hearing *The Jazz Singer* with Al Jolson—the first movie with sound. That was an unforgettable experience. Sound changed movies, from then on and going forward to unimaginable heights.

Seeing so many movies at a young age had a strong influence on my growing up. As mentioned, I wanted to be a pilot after seeing *The Dawn Patrol*. Whenever a young actor was shown attending military school, that also became my ambition. It was realized when I became an aviation cadet.

Seeing wealthy people and their lifestyle on the screen made this seem like something I should strive for. And I did, all through my growing up. All in all, the family adventure of going to the movies, many years ago, paved the way for all of my future ambitions to come true.

It was about this time in my life that I got to know my mother's sisters and brothers. I knew my aunts and uncles as all young children do, being spoiled by them at one time or another. However, growing up, in their own ways, each left me with an indelible memory of our loving relationships.

My Grandmother and Grandfather, in their day, had no radio or TV. So they seemed to keep busy having children. They had a brood of ten children: three boys and seven girls.

The photo in the insert shows six of the seven sisters: Aunt Fannie, the oldest, had passed away a few years earlier. Uncle Leo, the youngest, lived in Denver, Colorado.

For a number of years some of the sisters lived in the up-stairs apartment of our home, with my grandparents, until they married and moved on. Listening to their conversations about what they were wearing and what beauty salons they were going to, and all the talk of young women dressing, helped me to understand, later in my life as a retailer, what it was that women were interested in.

In the 20s and early 30s, though, the cousins would also get together at Manhattan Beach during the summer.

Of all the sisters, we were closest to Aunt Esther. She and Uncle Sam Silver moved upstairs in 488 East 35th Street after the other sisters married and moved away. They had two children, Irwin and Rena. Irwin was the same age as my older brother, Lester. We three were pals as we grew up.

Our greatest pleasure at the time was for our mothers to agree that Irwin, my brothers and I could play Monopoly on Sunday nights, and that Irwin could come upstairs after the game was over.

Aunt Esther would be proud to know that Irwin was a combat photographer during WWII. A few years later, when he became ill, he married his nurse, Anne Marie Baron. They have a wonderful family. One of Irwin's children, Mitchell Silver, became a New York City Parks Commissioner, a very prestigious and important government position.

Aunt Esther and my mother were great movie fans. Most Saturday afternoons they would take Irwin, Rena, my brothers, Lester and Bert, and me either to the Kenmore movie theater, or the Lowe's Kings, both located in Brooklyn within walking distance of the Dutch Reform Church, where Governor Peter Stuyvesant is buried. Quite a contrast from the old Dutch colony.

I believe it was seeing many of the movies showing the life styles of successful executives that helped me have the ambition to achieve success of my own.

Lester left school to become a Western Union Messenger. I left high school a few years later. Bert continued school and went on to become an aspiring actor.

When Uncle Leo and Aunt Tess visited New York City about 1926, my mother had a dinner party in their honor. Aunt Tess brought along her younger brother, an artist. He drew a charcoal drawing of me. Unfortunately, my cousin Ruth accidentally smeared the drawing. The artist took it home to repair. I never saw it again.

Sixty later, Andy Warhol made a charcoal drawing of me. That more than made up for the loss.

Jackie and I were very fortunate, in a number of ways, with my business associations with Beatrice Fox Auerbach, the owner of G. Fox & Co. in Hartford, and a similar association with B. Altman & Co. in New York. In both cases we were exposed to the best of operas and symphonies.

Beatrice Auerbach invited Jackie and me to the new Metropolitan Opera House at Lincoln Center, for its opening night performance of Puccini's La Fanciulla Del West on April 11, 1966. B. Altman, through the generosity of the B. Altman Foundation, had a permanent box at the Metropolitan Opera that was available to executives of B. Altman & Co. We often took advantage of it.

Exposure to how the audiences dressed then, compared to the very casual way audiences dress today, has taken away the elegance those glorious experiences deserve. Because of this, we stopped attending, with very few exceptions, these marvelous events.

To this retiree, the general public's so called casual dress at classics being presented at Lincoln Center and Broadway theaters, has, for want of a better word, degraded the events for me, to the point they are no longer enjoyable. As for the theatre, I recall sitting in a desirable orchestra seat next to a man wearing shorts and a tee shirt as if he were attending a baseball game. This extremely casual dressing has happened not once, but so often that we stopped attending the theatre as well.

Social scientists will say that I am prejudiced against people who possibly can't afford and don't want to dress properly at an upscale event. My opinion is anyone who can afford to buy a ticket for an upscale event, can afford to wear a pair of pants and a shirt.

As an older, successful retiree I have found it more relaxing to not travel to the city with the hope of enjoying a theatre event or a concert, only to have it ruined by being surrounded by attendees who either don't know or don't care how they present themselves for a special event.

Instead, I have found it most enjoyable and much more relaxing to use my large screen TV, in the comfort and luxury of our home, to watch concerts and operas on DVDs, or PBS, as well as many movies available on Netflix, Amazon, iTunes, TCM, and so on.

As for dinners in New York, large or small, in most cases, at the restaurants and dinner parties we frequent, most guests are more aware what is considered required dressing— which of course makes the event more enjoyable.

To sum up, in years past we lived in an environment a bit more formal in many ways than what is considered acceptable today.

To have and enjoy a successful retirement means, to me, as much relaxation and the least amount of irritation as possible. That does not mean that today's mores should change for me.

However, for me to have a successful and enjoyable retirement, there is no reason why I must observe and put up with what I consider bad or no taste in symphony halls, Broadway theatres and fine restaurants.

When I was very young I observed how my parents dressed. My father, in addition to the derby that he wore, also wore spats, fashionable in the early twenties. He always looked the part of a successful lawyer.

My mother, of course, being one of seven sisters who were always competing, was always the best dressed.

As young children, my brothers and I were always dressed in style of the times. I recall my brothers and I all wore berets, proper shorts in the summer, and knickers in the fall and winter. That is until the crash of The Great Depression.

Clothes for us then, and many others, became a secondary consideration. That is, until years later when I started to work at Bonwit Teller. Even at that early point in my career, it was from the exposure to executives of the company as well as to the well-dressed customers that I became acutely aware how dressing defines the person.

Exercise

About a hundred years ago, Chauncey Depew (1834-1928), a politician of his day said, "I get my exercise as a pall bearer to my friends who exercise." That remark was so comical I thought it came from a comedian like W.C. Fields. Needless to say, since then it has been proven scientifically, that exercise will help everyone live a longer and healthy life.

Exercise has always come to me naturally. Particularly being retired, I know this is no time to take it easy. Not when the opposite is necessary!

Early on, when I lived in Brooklyn and attended Public School 181, there were races sponsored by Public School Athletic League, PSAL The school would close the street where the school was located for racing contests with the students. I won every race that I entered and received the small PSAL medal that we attached to our belts. Of course those of us who had the most medals on our belts were the heroes of the day.

When I was a bit older and attended Columbia University night classes, I would practice before my classes on the track where Uris Hall stands today. One evening I was pacing another runner and doing quite well; however, after a number of laps, I was running out of steam when the other runner ran past me in burst of speed, completing two more laps. I Introduced myself to, I think I have his name right, Greg Rice, one of the champion track stars of that era.

After that, during WWII, I did quite well in the Army Air Corps racing competitions. Parenthetically, my father won a number of races when he was in the army and stationed in

Panama in 1915. However, I believe the exercise that best ben-
efitted me in middle age was walking. When I lived in Hart -
ford, each morning I would walk about two miles from my
home to my office at G. Fox & Co. When I arrived back in New
York, I would walk about half a mile each morning from Grand
Central Station to B. Altman & Co., and the same distance on
my way back to the station in the evening.

The biggest and best exercise came when I moved to
Bergdorf Goodman. A walk of a mile from Grand Central each
morning to Bergdorf, and a mile walk back to the station each
evening, for seventeen years, undoubtedly contributed to my
present good health.

Now I have been retired for close to 25 years and the
walk to work is not necessary. Walking nine holes playing golf
a few times a week worked for a while, though I now use a golf
cart. That bit of exercise seems to work pretty well.

During unseasonable weather, I ride my stationary bicycle two miles each day. Having a DVD player attached to my
bicycle, which allows me take courses in art, history, science,
and so on, is an added plus.

An aside: In 1948, shortly after returning home from
military service, an army friend of mine, Irwin Glusker, and
I decided a bicycle hostel trip through Europe would be a desirable vacation. However, that proved to be too long a vacation, and possibly too expensive, so we decided to bicycle from
Quebec to New York.

We rented bicycles in New York, took a train to Quebec,
and started south from there. I don't recall how long the trip
took, but we bicycled about 15 to 20 miles a day through what
seemed to feel like the French country side. Irwin speaking

French helped us with lodgings part of the way. I also remember being surprised, biking through Cape Cod, that it wasn't all downhill as it appeared to be on the map.

We finally gave up by the time we reached Greenwich, Connecticut. I don't recall if we took the train to New York or hitchhiked the rest of the way. At the very least we got the hostel trip over and done with.

Again, to sum up, as a happy and healthy retiree, it would seem to me that exercise is like putting money in the bank for the future of a healthy retirement.

Smoking

I started smoking cigarettes when I was about eighteen years old. Camels or Chesterfields had a gadget that allowed me to roll my own. I tried it and soon upgraded to buying a regular pack, which I smoked about once a day.

Smoking cigarettes seemed the proper thing to do. Every sophisticated movie star smoked in the movies and strong advertising helped to develop the smoking habit.

During WWII, smoking helped to calm my nerves, as it did for most of the guys I served with. The Army PX made it easy to afford them: a carton of any brand of cigarettes was a dollar and a single pack, ten cents. Sometimes it seemed more sophisticated to smoke a pipe, which I enjoyed. A good cigar came later in life.

When I was employed at G. Fox & Co. in the 1960s, I developed a severe cold with an accompanying cough. It was so severe that a nurse at the store recommended seeing my doctor and I did.

The doctor took an X-ray. As I recall, he asked me to wait until he studied the results. Much to my amazement and concern, he told me he didn't like what he saw and would take the X-ray again.

Well, you can imagine my great worry. Here I was in my forties, with a wife and two young children. I was too young to die. While waiting, I prayed to God and every Deity, please don't let this happen to me. On the spot, I promised to give up smoking.

He took the next X-ray. After studying it, he said it was fine, gave me some medication, and told me to stop smoking and go home and get into bed. He explained that this was a new X-ray machine and he had to learn how to use it. Sorry to have worried me.

It wasn't until a few years later that I realized my doctor had recognized smoking was a killer. He used this tactic on his patients to get them to give up smoking.

Both my wife and I gave up smoking "cold turkey." With a scare like that it wasn't too difficult.

As for our children, they learned at an early age that smoking was prohibited. It is family lore that when our youngest daughter Robin was about four or five years old, she saw me smoking and asked if she could try it. Of course I told her, in no uncertain terms, "No." However, she insisted, so to teach her a lesson, I let her have a puff of a cigarette. She choked and coughed, and kept hitting my foot, saying, "You are a very bad Daddy!" She learned her lesson. We still laugh about it.

Today with it being a proven fact that smoking is a killer, I come close to asking people I see smoking on the street, don't you know that you are committing suicide? However, I restrain myself and am thankful that my doctor of many years ago saved my life.

Liberal Arts

I always knew that I missed a great deal when it became necessary for me to leave high school and unfortunately, later on, I was not able to attend college in order to earn a proper degree.

The evening business courses at Columbia Business School, helpful as they were for my business career, contributed nothing toward my interest in liberal arts.

When I retired I found that I had the time and ambition to make up for what I had missed, a Liberal Arts education. During my lifetime, as mentioned previously, I read enough to be considered well read. However, art was a subject that I very much appreciated when I visited, with my wife, the great museums in the United States, Italy, Spain, France, England and Russia. Learning the history of great art and artists became my area of study during my years of retirement.

Very fortunately, modern technology took me beyond reading books about art and artists. On my "magic box" I am not only able to visit nearly all the museums in the world, but able to take virtual tours of many of them. Along with the great art of centuries past, I am also able to study impressionist and modern art.

In addition, as mentioned, I have been able to combine exercise with my art studies by using a DVD player attached to my stationary bicycle, while I am peddling away on my two miles each day.

When I lived in Flatbush, Brooklyn in the 30s, it was the same distance to walk to Ebbets Field, where the Brooklyn Dodgers played, as it was to walk to the Brooklyn Museum. Tickets to see a Saturday ballgame were about 50 cents to sit up in the center field bleachers, where I once caught a ball from the Dodgers' third baseman, Cookie Lavagetto.

On Sundays, I would walk to the Brooklyn Museum to attend the Sunday Concert Series.

The experiences helped me to appreciate sports as well as classical music.

Today the advantage of listening to the classics while writing on my computer, with any number of great DVDs available, plus links like Pandora or WQXR has answered my desire for the music I learned to love when I was very young.

To sum up; I found missed opportunities can always be retrieved when there exists a desire and the time to do so.

Keeping Up to Date

Going back to when I was very young, the newspapers delivered to our home were *The New York Times*, which my father took with him to his office, *The Daily News* and the *Journal American*. My brothers and I spent hours going through the comic strips from both of those newspapers. The Sunday comics were so important that when there was a newspaper strike before WWII, Mayor LaGuardia read the comics over the radio in order for the children of New York not to miss a beat.

Today of course, in New York City, everything about the news and newspapers has changed, except for the venerable *Women's Wear Daily*, *The New York Times* and *The Wall Street Journal*. *The New York Post* and *The Daily News* continue as tabloids, but all the other daily newspapers of that era, like the ocean liners of the past, are gone.

Now these many years later, as a retiree, I still have an insatiable appetite for news of the day—as much, if not more than I did back when I looked forward to reading the comics.

Having a routine to cover the news has been very help-ful, keeping me and Jackie up to date as to what is going on in the world. Delivery of *The New York Times* to our front door, each and every morning, makes reading the important news at breakfast an enjoyable ritual. The rest of the *Times* is saved for later in the day, to be read at my leisure.

After breakfast, on my computer I have the following to scan online: *Women's Wear Daily, The Wall Street Journal*, Politico, Reuters, The Huffington Post, *The Financial Times,* and Bloomberg News. Keeping up to date as to what is going on around you can enjoyably take up most of the morning.

Reading the balance of the *Times,* followed by a short nap in the late afternoon, is a great way for me to complete an enjoyable day of retirement. For any current news happening that day, there are any number of evening news channels on TV that can bring me up to date.

To Sum up: In addition to the many activities mentioned above, to me a successful and enjoyable retirement means be-ing able to do what I want to do, when I want to do it. I have found keeping up with what is going on in the world around me keeps my mind active and challenged. It would be unwise for me to be inactive. I am not interested allowing my mind to slow down in boredom.

Driving

As previously mentioned, having a financial planner in my life helped to bring about certain luxuries that, earlier in my life, I might not have thought necessary.

As an example: I have always been interested, as we used to say, in automobiles. My mother called them machines. My father back in 1928, before the Great Depression, as mentioned, had a Marmon, an upscale luxury car of that era. In those days automobiles came in three colors: black, blue and maroon. Mother's favorite color was lavender. That being the case, the Marmon was painted lavender. It really stood out.

Father also had a Chevrolet with a rumble seat for my brothers and I to accompany him when he visited his clients. The Marmon was mother's. On weekends, father would take the whole family for a drive in the Marmon. Sometimes we went as far as Lakehurst, New Jersey to see the new dirigibles. They were a sight to behold.

Years later, when I was about eighteen, two friends and I bought an old Ford. Not a Model T, but close to it. The car was so old that I think the registration cost us more than the car. I recall driving over the Brooklyn Bridge when the gearshift pulled out and had to be quickly shoved back into place.

During the war, I had a Jeep at my disposal on Saipan. But my real driving experiences began when I moved from New York City to Providence, Rhode Island. Today, driving 160 miles using I 95, the trip takes about two and a half hours. Before 95, using Routes 6 and 44 was about the same distance. But the traveling time was over four hours.

My driving experiences from Gladdings in Providence, where I was a merchandise manager, was a long haul. Leaving each week on Saturday, at six in the evening and driving to New York City to meet with my buyers in their markets Monday morning, was a chore. However, as I found out in life, when you get familiar with a procedure, pleasant or not, you become used to it. Once in a while I would take the sleeper to NY. One evening in the waiting room of the Providence railroad station I saw a tall, good-looking young man, Senator Jack Kennedy waiting for his driver. Later, when I moved to Hartford, Connecticut, my weekly driving trips were shorter, but still a chore.

Finally, when I moved back to New York, through my employer B. Altman & Co., I was entitled to have a car to drive to visit the branch stores each week. They asked what type of care did I need or want. When I requested a Jaguar, the management of that ultra conservative company practically had to have a board meeting.

My reason for selecting the Jaguar was due to B. Altman sending me around the world to meet all their commissionaires.

My first stop was in Hawaii. In addition to meeting B. Altman's bathing suit manufacturer, I visited an old friend, from Gladdings, George Ladd who lived there. George had a beautiful vintage Jaguar that I fell in love with. As I moved on to Japan, I checked out all the Japanese cars, as I did in Germany, France and, finally, England.

Jaguar was the car for me, even though B. Altman management didn't understand why a Buick wouldn't do to get me to the branches. The reason for my long driving history is to make the point, that as a retiree with limited driving needs. I have grown to dislike driving any long distances. I also dislike driving beyond my immediate living area at night

My recommended solution to the problem came about when I became aware of off-duty policemen who were interested in supplementing their income by driving my newest Jaguar. Not only are they knowledgeable about traffic problems and how to get to where I want to go, they are professionals who know how to drive and handle traffic situations. And they are gentlemen at all times.

Is using drivers a luxury? Yes. However, with business and social trips necessary from Westchester where I live to New York City and beyond, this is a well-earned luxury for this retiree. For those who live and work in the cities, Uber and other services are very helpful for getting around.

Doctors, Medicine and Good Health

During a lifetime, all types of illnesses and accidents will occur. Having a doctor's, early diagnosis, proper medicines and treatment available I have found, will go a long way, in many cases, to help get through medical problems.

In my case, I was struck with scarlet fever at an early age—about three or four years old. In those days, before antibiotics, scarlet fever was fatal in many cases. All I remember was being sick in bed for a long time and that our home was quarantined. With luck and proper medical care, I got through that. I then had all the normal childhood diseases of that time, mumps, measles, and so on.

I also had accidents that required stitches. While playing at home I banged my head on a radiator, That required our neighborhood doctor to make a house call to close the wound.

Next, as the last roller skater in line of four or five other kids, I was whipped past a tree where my left foot caught the wire wrapped around a tree. I came very close to severing my Achilles tendon. Once again, our doctor's house call patched me up.

House calls, having a doctor come to your home when needed, I am sorry to say, are a thing of the past.

I mention those medical experiences since that was, I believe, the norm for my generation.

My next medical experience was enlisting in the Army Air Corps in 1942. To qualify to be an Aviation Cadet, a rigid physical was required. I was so underweight that I ate three or four bananas before my exam. I passed all the physical requirements except for my being under weight. The medical officer who stamped my forms said, "You pass. You will put on the required weight in the Air Corps."

He was wrong. I was the same weight when I came out, as I was when I went in.

Again, for me and my generation of retirees, the medical problems of our early years have fortunately been overcome by advances in medicine.

But it is in middle age and beyond when the wheels begin to fall off. I won't go into any of my physical problems that, at some time or other, began to show up, other than to say that quick recognition, and a quick visit to my doctors when something doesn't feel or seem right, is like first aid. It would seem that early recognition of a problem and early treatment minimizes medical problems down the road.

To sum up, I found that for me to be a healthy retiree it is as important to have a doctor, or doctors, available for consultation on whatever it is that ails me, as it is to have other advisors who have helped me achieve a healthy life style.

I believe it was Winston Churchill who said,"Growing old isn't for cowards."

Taking good care of you helps you *not*tobeacoward.

Sleep

When I was very young growing up in Brooklyn, sleep, as I recall, was never a problem. I am sure it is the same for all children. As a matter of fact, many times when my mother said, "Lights out," I would have a flashlight with me to read under the blanket, until I was tired enough to go to sleep.

Another activity of mine, under the blanket when I was supposed to be sleeping, was experimenting with my crystal set. A crystal set was an early radio receiver that picked up radio signals without electricity. It was a small crystal, using wire as thin as a cat's whisker moved around until a station was picked up to hear on my earphones.

I had an antenna hooked up from my bedroom window to the roof of our garage and would search for radio transmissions within a couple hundred miles—possibly as far as Boston and Philadelphia. For a young boy, it was another miracle of that age. Fortunately, as the years went by, I rarely had a problem sleeping, which may be a reason for longer life.

Which brings me to an article on sleeping that I recently read in *The New York Times*.

Maiken Nedergaard, a Danish biologist said; "As our body sleeps our brains are clearing out all the junk that has accumulated as a result of our daily thinking."

Hopefully, that is true. I am not a scientist or a doctor, thus not in a position to advise others that a good night's sleep is required for a successful and happy retirement. I can only say, at my advanced age, that a good night's sleep is a blessing.

Once in a while, if I find it difficult to fall asleep, or I can't get back to sleep, I try to relax and think about playing a few holes of golf, or a movie I just saw. It seems to work.

Beer, Wine and Whisky

My earliest exposure to alcohol was in 1933 when prohibition was repealed. I was 12 years old. Beer was approved to have 3.2 percent alcohol. My friends and I were able to get a few bottles of beer and marveled at the fact "we could feel getting high." That began and ended that early, enjoyable experiment.

I always had a few beers after work when I went bowling with the Bonwit Teller parking attendants, when I was the assistant to the doorman. The doorman himself, Pat Reilly, would ask me to go to a delicatessen on Sixth Avenue to buy two quart bottles of beer for him. I was smart enough to let him imbibe, while I took care of the door.

When I was promoted to the office boy to the president, I was periodically invited to attend retail industry events. To be sure I would not let an alcohol highball make me forget myself before the event, I would stop of in Halpert's drugstore down 56th Street for a milkshake. I was told that would neutralize the drink. I guess it did, since I received one more promotion to the merchandise office before I left for the Army Air Corps.

It was in the Air Corps that I learned moderation was the best approach to drinking.

I was stationed on Saipan with the 20th Air Force and beer was rationed. However, there was always an ample supply. Since the best way to drink beer is very cold, putting a case of beer in the bomb bay of a B29 on a training mission always did the trick. Whiskey was also rationed, but available. This provided me with an early lesson on overindulgence.

When the Japanese surrendered, I was able to get a bottle of Southern Comfort and celebrated. Unfortunately, Southern Comfort being so smooth, I drank more than enough to realize that heavy drinking was not for me. I am not sure how I got back to my quarters, but I made it.

Waiting to go home I found a way to transfer to an Air Sea Rescue Squadron, which moved me to Hawaii, getting me closer to home and possibly an earlier discharge. While there I frequented a restaurant called P. Y. Chong (mentioned in the book, *Unbroken*). While at the bar, I made the mistake of cashing the Christmas check from Bonwit Teller.

My concern, about what would happen if my employer found that I was drinking on their money, taught me to be aware of what I was doing after a drink as well as before. (I never heard back from Bonwit Teller).

In 1950, when I was the blouse buyer for Bonwit Teller, I met and became friendly with Geoffrey Beene, who eventually became a world renown fashion designer. Once in a while we would meet at the bar in the Plaza Hotel. We would order a martini or two and a stinger.

This I would not recommend at any age. The hangover was not worth the pleasure.

My travels around the world led me to drink the specialties of each country. Japan is where I had my first Japanese lunch—at the Okura hotel in Tokyo, with Mr. Hondo, the ninety year old representative from B. Altman's buying office. When he was young man, he took Mr. Altman to fine Japanese restaurants. Following Mr. Altman were other B. Altman executives. Now it was my turn. I fell in love with traditional Japanese food, which was made more enjoyable with a wonderful cup of saki or two, or three.

On buying trips to Ireland, the most enjoyable times were when, along the way, we would stop at various pubs for lunch. That is where I learned to enjoy Guinnes Stout.

Scotland, where I visited various cashmere houses—Lyle and Scott, Pringle, Ballantine, etc.—is where I learned to cultivate a taste for scotch. Particularly Scotland's favorite and mine, Famous Grouse.

I was introduced to English gin on my first visit to the Connaught Hotel in 1967. The Connaught had the best steak dining room in London, and great gin and tonics. That was the year Harrods opened their Way In Shop, and Biba had all the girls were wearing short skirts. It was a site to behold for a New England retailer.

Italy's wonderful wines always started when my flights arrived in Milan in time for lunch. I will always remember the waiter's first question, "Red or white and water with gas?"

Each and every restaurant was better and better, until I visited Harry's Bar in Venice. That, for me, in Italy, was the ultimate. I was so taken with the restaurant that I invited Arigio Cipriani to open a Harry's Bar on Bergdorf Goodman's newly renovated seventh floor. He declined, saying he didn't plan to come to New York. However, three years later, Arigio opened Cipriani with great success in the Sherry Netherland Hotel across Fifth Avenue from Bergdorf. I always felt that Berg-dorf Goodman benefited from his move. The ladies who lunch would have their lunch at Cipriani then cross Fifth Avenue to shop at Bergdorf.

Meanwhile, I needed all the space I could get to add departments for our rapidly growing business.

In France, I learned about fine wines. The Hotel Ritz was, for me, always the best. Auberges throughout the south of France gave me the opportunity to try the best wines of Bordeaux and Burgundies.

In my visits to Germany and Austria I learned about fine beers. The different brews available amazed me. Beer today is still my favorite alcoholic drink, particularly when I am thirsty.

Visiting the fur auctions in Leningrad, I was introduced Russia's vodka with dollops of caviar. That was a memorable experience.

For safety I away stayed with bottled beer for my trips to India.

Scotch was safe to drink as long as it came straight from the bottle, with no ice cubes, please.

As mentioned, I learned early on that drinking in moderation is the best way to enjoy, beer, wine and whisky. I never forgot it.

Now, as a retiree, I of course drink in moderation. However, a bit of alcohol—beer, wine or whiskey—before and during a meal is an enjoyable habit that I look still forward to.

Relationships

Being retired allows me a great deal of time to think about a lifetime of relationships. There are in my opinion, three relationships that are important to every individual, retired or otherwise.

Family, friends and business, in that order.

Family relationships as we all know, are instilled at an early age. How one is brought up in a family of loving and attentive parents, goes a long way to forming a person's personality.

The greatest decision that affects us for the rest of our lives is falling in love and selecting the person to marry. Since in many cases this is a lifelong commitment, a great deal of thought has to be given before making this decision. A solid family background and support does not guarantee a happy and successful marriage, but it helps a great deal.

When I met my wife I was thirty years old. As did all young men of my time, I'd had a number of romances, but nothing substantial enough for me to make a commitment. When I met Jackie Myers I knew, on our first date, that this was the woman I would marry.

Very fortunately, Jackie's reaction was the same as mine. We were, after a brief courtship, married six months later.

The point here, I believe, is both Jackie and I, at our mature ages, had seen enough of dates and life to make us feel that we would have a true and long lasting love. Love to last a long lifetime.

Since these pages are to explain how I came to have a successful and happy retirement, a successful and loving marriage should be regarded as the foundation for all that was to come. I believe, in addition to loving each other, Jackie and I have found it is imperative to have respect for each other. In the dictionary there is a long list defining respect. The one I like best: "To be admired and respected."

It would seem that if you love, admire and respect your marriage partner throughout life, the bumps in the road are diminished, making the odds for a successful and happy marriage very high.

Social Relationships

Relationships with friends also start very early in life. Unfortunately, as we grow from young children having friends in school and in our neighborhoods, this is but a transient period in life. Not very long lasting, but formative.

My friends early on all lived in my neighborhood. We played stick ball together, raced our homemade box carts and later joined the Boy Scouts. While being a Boy Scout was another defining moment in my lifetime, no long lasting friend - ships emerged from that experience.

Later, in high school and college, some relationships can last a lifetime. Since I didn't attend college, this was not an experience that I was able to enjoy.

My first real friendships began during and after my Air Corps service. I was stationed at Boca Raton, Florida for a period of time before I went overseas. There, I had a group of fellow radar instructors and we spent our weekends together.

One bit of luck was, as mentioned, Aunt Bert and Uncle Eddie having a home in Miami Beach. They very generously invited me and a friend or two to spend our weekend leaves at their home. I tried keeping in touch with some of them. But life moved on too fast for me to do more than an occasional dinner with one good friend who would visit from Chicago once a year.

Another army friend, Irwin Glusker, lives in New York. We keep in touch through writing letters, the old fashion way.

Even the names listed at the beginning of this memoir, the aviation cadets who served with me, are a distant memory. I am sure other retirees who served in WWII have the same regret at not being able to keep ongoing relationships with long ago friendships.

Social friendships, I have found, have the ability to last a longer time. If for no other reason than wives seem to be more social creatures than men.

After marrying Jackie in Providence, we had a circle of young friends. But when we moved to Hartford, we lost the friends in Providence and made new friends in Hartford. We had the same experience when we moved from Hartford to New York.

I am sure I am not that much different from other business retirees who had to move from city to city following their career paths.

I do recall a summer evening when I attended a dinner party at our country club, Tumblebrook, in Bloomfield, Con - necticut. Standing outside, under a star studded sky, I remember thinking, as happy as my wife, I and our children are living here, one day we will be moving on.

Moving on, losing friends and making new ones is the penalty and enjoyment of successful business executives, leading to a happy retirement. I mention Tumblebrook near West Hartford, Connecticut; Ledgemont in Seekonk, Massachusetts; and Century Country Club in Westchester, New York. It is most important, if possible, to join a club—golf, tennis, sailing, swimming, hunting, and so on.

These are the country clubs Jackie and I have had the good fortune to belong to, that not only rounded out our lives when we were younger, but have brought about lifelong friendships, that we enjoy today.

Business Relationships

For me it would seem, business relationships in a few cases lasted the longest. The reason: I am still in contact with people whom I did business with going back many years. Actually, going back to the 1950s. This comes about by moving from store to store, but still doing business with many of the same people.

Some are friends, others acquaintances of long standing.

As much as I regret losing the friendships of my long time ago Army friends, a similar experience of losing a close business friend came about by my neglecting (forgetting) to invite him and his wife to the opening party of Bergdorf Goodman's Men's Store. This very unfortunate mistake caused the casualty of a longtime friendship

In summary, good and happy relationships with family, friends and business associates are imperative for a successful and happy retirement. My maintaining and continuing to build relationships is and should be a never-ending goal, even in retirement.

Summary

Now that I have listed and written about my many "desirable priorities" required for a successful and happy retirement, let me describe their total benefits toward an enjoyable social life.

I have found my loving wife and loving children, throughout much of my life, to be the bedrock of my happiness. Adding to that is the wonder and blessing of grandchildren. Watching each grandchild grow to reach their potential is really one of my great rewards reached during retirement. Knowing that all are well and going about their business of schools, jobs and careers frees up the mind to enjoy every day as a gift to be enjoyed by participating in a social life with family and friends. To enjoy all and any of what I have listed here as lifetime priorities.

To sum up:

My good fortune for a successful and happy retirement is my loving and devoted wife, our children, Janie and Robin, and our fabulous grandchildren. As mentioned earlier, a loving wife made it all possible.

My wife, Jackie, and my daughters Janie and Robin have made my retirement a joy. All through my children's growing up into and during my retirement, my daughters have made every day I spent with them a happy, exhilarating and loving experience.

I keep my daughters' photographs and their children's— Janie's children Russ, Pam and Betsy; and Robin and Fred's children Hallie and Mallory—on my desk to constantly remind me of the joy and happiness they have brought to me over my long lifetime.

As I finish this chapter, I have just been notified that Jackie and I have become great grandparents. Emily, Russell's wife, gave birth this morning to a baby boy. The little boy's room at the hospital is 720. Next door to 721. Would you believe it?

The backyard pond I created in summer and winter. With fish added, it became a giant aquarium.

Camping in Bear Mountain on the Appalachian Trail, about 1937

Golf at Windsor Castle as a guest of Princess Diana

Flying was another
early passion

Grandson Russ on the True Love

Jackie and I in the front row at Lincoln Center with Les and
Fan Samuels

Photos are a wonderful way to document the major and minor events of life!

Photo of me with my father when I was about 6 months years old and another, when I was about 10 years old

My grandparents had 10 children: three boys, seven girls.
The photo shows six of the sisters. Aunt Fannie, the oldest,
had passed away. Uncle Leo, the youngest, lived in Denver.

In the 20s and early 30s, the cousins would get together at
Manhattan Beach. *Top Row*: Mother, Uncle Jack
Second row: Aunt Mary, cousins, Lilly, Rosalyn, Sylvia, Aunt
Rose *Bottom row*: Cousin Ruth, Brothers, Lester, Bert and Ira

Mother, brothers Lester and Bert and me

Father with Lester about 1919

Sitting on the "running board"
of Mother's Marmon

Soft ball was a sport that I enjoyed playing

On Sundays, I would walk to the Brooklyn Museum to attend the Sunday Concert Series.

Father joined the Army before WWI, I believe to see the
world.

Epilogue

Jackie put many albums together from the many newspaper articles of my long retail career.

They start with a photo from *Women's Wear Daily* of Randy Stambaugh, who, when he was promoted to president of B. Altman & Co. in 1970, recommended me to be vice president and general merchandise manager. This allowed me to resign, with pleasure, from that same position at G. Fox & Co. in Hartford, Connecticut, then owned by The May Co.

This move brought me to the attention of Carter Hawley Hale which bought Bergdorf Goodman in 1972.

After Carter Hawley Hale had owned Bergdorf Goodman for three years, Phil Hawley, the president, hired me to become the CEO and president of that fine store. Without Randy Stambaugh bringing me back to New York this remarkable story would have never happened.

When FAO Schwartz moved across 58th Street to the then General Motors building, their location in the then Squib building became available to BG. We moved Bergdorf's men's division across Fifth Avenue to three times the space it had previously had in the women's store, making Bergdorf Goodman's Men's Store the largest men's store on Fifth Avenue.

The objectives and strategies for Bergdorf Goodman were based on my experience working at Bonwit Teller in the 1940s: Give the luxury customer what she wants. Fifty years later the same business principals worked. Great assortments of fashion merchandise. The comfortable environment that this customer is used to and expects. Customer service beyond comparison.

Once the strategy of updating Bergdorf Goodman from an old, expensive and intimidating retailer, to a young, intimidating and expensive retailer was put into place, the positioning of knowledgeable merchandisers, and the growth in sales and profits at Bergdorf increased dramatically,

The main strategy was to convert the store from old, dull, expensive and intimidating to young exciting, expensive and intimidating. We catered to the woman who went to the best restaurants, best hotels and best resorts, and belonged to the best clubs. The same customer strategy applied to Bergdorf Goodman's Men's Store.

This might be the place for me to give my opinion regarding the state of retailing at the end of the 20th century and the beginning of the 21st. It is based on my experiences. I was exposed to the retail businesses as a young child—often shopping with my mother, later with my wife and two daughter—and my own 60 plus year career as a retailer spanned three different states, three department stores and three specialty stores

The retail devastation began with the demise of all the Frederick Atkins stores (except Dillard's) and of many, many other family owned stores during the seventies and eighties. Today, with the failing of Macy's, Sears Roebuck, and too many others to name, it is imperative to go back to the beginning of successful traditional retailing. And to recognize the changes that took place—failures too many retailers failed to recognize, causing the closing of so many retail businesses

It is also important to remember that many successful retailers who thrived during the late nineteenth century into the twentieth century, started as peddlers, going from door to door. They conveniently offered merchandise that their customers wanted. There were, of course, retail stores in existence, such as Jordan Marsh in Boston; Macy's in New York; Marshall

Field in Chicago; Harrods in London; and Galleries Lafayette in Paris, to name a few. There was even the Sears Roebuck catalog, the first direct mail operation that delivered merchandise to customers all over the country. Later Sears opened brick and mortar stores—not unlike Amazon's experiment begun in 2016.

Basic to all these successful retail ventures: they sold the merchandise customers wanted when they wanted it.

Whether by peddlers coming to their doors, catalogs delivered by mail, or in department stores with tremendous assortments, customers found what they wanted. And, of course, most importantly, there were professional salespeople to help customers select merchandise. The ability of these professionals to sell additional merchandise to those customers (multiple selling) was also important.

This happy and very successful world of retailing slowly, but surely began to unravel. First were the discount retailers, such as Lohemann's Filenes Basement, and a few others—forerunners of the New England mill outlets—which opened in the sixties. This led to the beginning of Walmart and soon spurred the discount revolution.

In addition to the great discounters spreading across the country, large shopping malls also began opening across the country. These developments, of course, left no room for the popular, family owned stores to exist.

Next, with discount stores growing, too many stores expanded beyond profitability. Eventually, shopping malls weakened, due to the Internet, and brick and mortar stores began experiencing further declines.

It would seem that most retailers in the latter part of the 20th century and the beginning of the 21st began moving toward self-service; so much so that many apparel retail stores were called rack city. Also, as many retailers began extending sales hours, one of the main ingredients of successful retailing, professional sales people, were minimized or eliminated.

Worse, in order to maintain sales volume, many retailers became addicted to off price sales, if not every day, then every week.

I use the word addicted since, like dope addicts, once hooked on off price sales, retailers found it is nearly impossible to go back to being regular price retailers. Customers then began to consider off price merchandise as the norm.

This left all types of retailing, except luxury retailers to a lesser degree, open to the competition of the Internet. Or e-commerce.

Those brick and mortar stores that serve as warehouses for brands and designer merchandise (see Macy's) were overwhelmed by e-commerce. Customers found it much easier to shop at home or the office, or on their computer or cellphone.

As a good example, I mention luxury retailers, such as Hermès of Paris where I served as a director for more than twenty years. Hermès sales and profits have increased year after year. Even during the holiday season of 2016, a disappointment to almost all retailers, Hermès continued to have a successful season.

Those retailers who are able to create a "buying experience," plus great customer service, and great assortments of new and exciting merchandise will continue in business. E-commerce in many cases, will be part of their sales, as is, and has been, direct mail.

In the latter part of the twentieth century, e-commerce, with its shopping convenience and large and broad merchandise assortments immediately delivered to the customer's door, moved into the place occupied by local stores, as well as large brick and mortar stores. Also, a great number of discount retailers found an abundant number of customers.

Last, the complete cycle for all customers, young and old, is filled with the basics of retailing:

A. Brick and mortar retailers, who provide the "buying experience," plus great assortments of merchandise and outstanding customer service. (See Nordstrom's.) Will continue with success.
B. E-commerce providing large assortments of merchandise, delivered immediately, with little or no customer service.
C. Discount stores, too many to be listed here. In many cases, replacing the family owned stores, in every neighborhood.

Retailing hasn't changed; it is still selling wanted merchandise to customers of all ages.

It has evolved into different methods of distribution. It's no longer just department and family owned stores, as listed in Frederick Atkins, that supply wanted merchandise. E-commerce and discount retailers have filled the gap, replacing the dominance of the department and family owned stores

This method of retail evolution will, in my opinion, continue into the future with the steps listed above, as the A-B-C of retailing.

Newspaper clippings showing the rise of Bergdorf Goodman in becoming the major fashion retailer on Fifth Avenue

Without Randy Stambaugh bringing me back to New York this remarkable story would have never happened.

This letter from Frank Savage to Randy Stambaugh reminded me of when I was the office boy to William H. Holmes, president of Bonwit Teller in1940.

Frank L. Savage Inc
REPRESENTATIVES & IMPORTERS

Alan Paine

Cable: RANK FIRST NEW YORK
Telephone: (212) 679-1600

17 EAST 37th STREET
NEW YORK, N. Y. 10016

August 5, 1969

Mr. Randolph Stambaugh
B. Altman & Co.
Fifth Avenue at 34th Street
New York, New York 10016

Dear Randy,

When I returned from vacation yesterday, our mutual friend, Alec Marchbank, told me that Ira Neimark had joined your company as General Merchandise Manager.

I feel that it is correct on my part to send you my congratulations on securing this gentleman, whom I have known since the early days when he was working as an assistant to the late Mr. William Holmes of Bonwit Teller. There is no doubt in my mind that he will prove to be a powerful asset in your organization.

Trusting this finds you fit and well, and with kindest regards,

Yours sincerely,

Frank

FLS/du

For WWD to say, "Bergdorf Goodman is what it is today largely because of Ira Neimark" is the supreme compliment.

August 14, 2012

Ira Neimark's Founding Vision

By DAVID MOIN

Bergdorf Goodman is what it is today largely because of Ira Neimark.

In 1975, Neimark became chairman and chief executive officer of Bergdorf's when the store had sagged to second-rate status and was overshadowed by Bloomingdale's, Saks Fifth Avenue and Barneys New York. But Neimark, with a strong team and a clear vision, was able to transform Bergdorf's into a world-class bastion of luxury labels and prestigious designer collections. Its reputation hasn't wavered since he retired from the store in 1992.

"When I joined Bergdorf Goodman, it was a very small business run by a family. There was an unimaginable opportunity for a store in that location, with luxury customers living up and down Fifth Avenue and up and down Park Avenue," Neimark said.

Ira Neimark
Photo By Thomas Iannaccone

Working with Dawn Mello, the fashion director, and Steve Elkin, the chief financial officer, he developed a strategy to get designers to sell Bergdorf's at a time when they would only sell the competition. It involved promising them prominent in-store shops with greater square footage than other stores provided. It also involved buying the couture collections from certain designers such as Yves Saint Laurent, Givenchy and Christian Dior, a move practically unheard of among fashion retailers in the U.S. But Neimark saw the tactic as a means to not only put the spotlight on Bergdorf's but also as a way to gain access to these designers' ready-to-wear lines that Bergdorf's sorely lacked.

RELATED STORY: The Tenure of Burt Tansky >>

Neimark firmly believed that designers should be lavished with attention and that Bergdorf's would bask in the afterglow. "We promoted the very devil out of every up-and-coming designer, so they became highly recognizable. We were the last guy on the block with them. Barneys had them. Saks had them. Bloomingdale's had them, and Bendel's had them. So we had these major fashion shows by the fountain at The Plaza hotel or the ice skating rink at Rockefeller Center, for Fendi, Calvin Klein, others. We promoted designers to such a degree they felt they were more important in many cases than retailers."

Neimark would also acknowledge that, sometimes, more money was spent promoting the designers than on

Ribbon Cutting Ceremony for the opening of Bergdorf
Goodman's Men's Store in September 1990

Many articles on the change in Bergdorf's management and
strategies appeared in fashion, and financial papers.

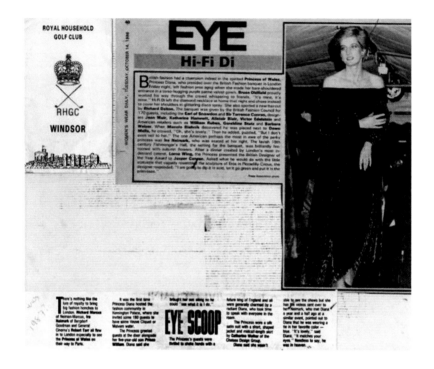

The October 1986 news article about my being seated to the right of Princess Diana at a fashion awards dinner in London was another wonderful experience never to be forgotten.

February 9th
1996.

Dear Mr Neimark,

I was enormously touched by your lovely letter & I wanted to thank you & your wife so much for thinking of me during this difficult time.

I recall very well our two meetings with fond memories,

but you forgot to include (!)
the discussion we had
about a British designer, Bruce
Oldfield who we thought
might have brought his
talent to Bergdorf Goodman;
no lapse of memory from this
lady I fear!

Thank you, more than I
can possibly say, for sharing
such kindness in writing to
me — Your words brought a
great deal of comfort . . . .
With my love to you both.
from. Diana.

Letter from Princess Diana thanking Jackie and me for our
letter to her during her
"difficult time"

The Fifth Avenue CEOs

courtesy of *Harpers Bazaar*

George Bayliss, Bonwit Teller; Ira Neimark Bergdorf
Goodman; Marvin Traub, Bloomingdales; John Christian,
B. Altman; Harry Murray, Lord & Taylor; Norman
Wechsler, I Magnin; HarryPlatt, Tiffany

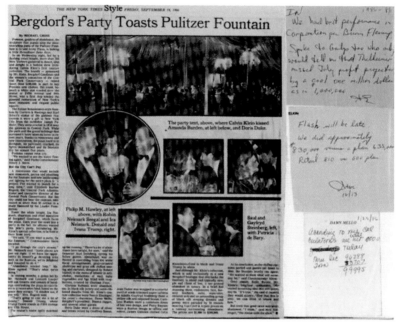

Bergdorf's Party Toasts Pulitzer Fountain

The party tent, above, where Calvin Klein kissed Amanda Burden, at left below, and Doris Duke.

Philip M. Hawley, at left above, with Robin Neimark Bengal and Ira Neimark. Donald and Ivana Trump, right.

Saul and Gayfryd Steinberg, left, with Patricia de Bary.

September 1986 Bergdorf Goodman held a fashion show introducing our own Calvin Klein's exclusive "couture collection" at The Pulitzer Fountain, Central Park.

The Eye in WWD was always a highlight of what was going on in retailing. Above was a farewell dinner for Norman Wechsler leaving to be the president of I. Magnin, featuring Bill Arnold and Polly Bergen.

Followed by high profile fashion executives exiting Orsini's restaurant, featuring Geraldine Stutz, head of Bendel; Helen Galland, head of Bonwit Teller; Lucy Newhouse and Ira Neimark.

One of the first articles regarding Bergdorf Goodman introducing the Paris Couture to New York in 1978

Yves Saint Laurent's Pierre Berge giving permission for YSL'S couture line to be shown and sold at Bergdorf Goodman encouraged Hubert Givenchy and Dior's Jacque Rouet to do the same. This was the masterstroke that brought Bergdorf Goodman to the attention of the fashion industry and the fashion press.

WOMEN'S WEAR DAILY, FRIDAY, AUGUST 20, 1976

...amps Bergdorf to unlock store's potential

Continued From Page One

Bergdorf's, which, in 1975 reportedly did about $36,500,000 in its Fifth Ave. store and $7,250,000 in its White Plains unit, is expected to hit $39 million to $40 million in the flagship store in 1976, with White Plains drawing between $8 million and $8,500,000.

The store has always had its own cachet, based on an unwavering reputation for quality, taste and service. In the '60s, however, some market observers feel Bergdorf's lost sight of what was happening. As one put it, "During the entire sportswear explosion, they went on selling dresses."

Bergdorf's is still going to sell dresses, but it also plans to sell a lot of other categories. Some of the additions to the store include the first Fendi boutique in the U.S., a

[photo caption:] Ira Neimark

Geoffrey Beene shop, a comprehensive third-floor sportswear department and a carefully edited contemporary floor.

Perhaps more important, though, is the reorganization of departments, resulting in proper merchandise for underdeveloped departments, a more logical placement of certain categories and the shifting of others to better traffic locations.

The Tiktiner shop, for instance, which pulls a volume in the area of $1 million, is being enlarged and moved to a high-traffic spot.

them together makes for greater impact. Too, it is felt the designer salon salesperson is not geared to selling separates but is superb when it comes to selling dresses and this factor, plus the customer type drawn to this area, is expected to maximize the sportswear explosion.

The third floor is where the enlarged and relocated Tiktiner shop will be, leading into a completely new traditional sportswear department with such designers as Klein, Calvin Klein, Blassport and Kasper, J.L. Sport as well as imported sportswear. This replaces a rather lackluster rainwear department and better coats which will drop to four, along with a better-suit department. Also new to three will be a Christian Dior collection, a casual-coat category and separates.

Nov. 1 is the target date for completion of the renovated fourth floor although Neimark takes issue with the restricted implications of "renovation" and says, "Anybody can redo a floor. What we're trying to do is present the feeling of the merchandise."

To do this on four, Bergdorf's removed a wig department, consolidated gifts further back on the floor, placed linens and domestics in a previously unused space and also moved bridal back.

This freed a sizable space around the corner from the designer salon for a new better-dress department and, again, makes a sensible continuation for customers of these categories. Neimark says, "We feel there is a great potential for better-dress business." Price range for better dresses is $150 to around $400 with Kasper for Joan Leslie, Jerry Silverman, Mollie Parnis Boutique and Gloria Vanderbilt among resources.

Miss Bergdorf remains on five, relatively unchanged from its original concept as the place daughters went to shop while their mothers bought couture. A Richard Assatly boutique will be added.

Bergdorf's new sixth floor will be dedicated to the pure contemporary customer with apparel, accessories, shoes, even gifts, chosen carefully and specifically for this type of woman. Bob Barth, divisional merchandise manager for this area, as well as Ira and Miss Bergdorf, says Bergdorf's entry into a contemporary customer who is "smaller in size and likes the French cut" as opposed to Miss Bergdorf's customer — "the bulgy lady updated."

Size as well as life style defines this customer, Bergdorf people say. Dawn Mello, vice-president and fashion director, says, "This customer would spend $250 for a sweatercoat without thinking about it. She might

"Anybody can redo a floor. What we're trying to do is

Neimark acts to unlock BG's sales potential

By MARY MERRIS

NEW YORK — "It's easy to make a lot of changes within six months and say, 'Look, I'm dancing,'" says Ira Neimark.

Instead, Neimark, who took over the presidency of Bergdorf Goodman 18 months ago, has waited until now to complete a substantial number of changes that are affecting the look, merchandise and structure of most of the store's departments. And Neimark thinks this is the surest way of developing the potential of this specialty store.

See NEIMARK, page 5

TODAY

Nancy Reagan: After the fall

— Eye View, page 36

Connolly is president . . . at Gimbels-New York

— Page 2

Halston V shifting from sportswear to dresses

— Page 26

Donald Fisher set to bridge The Gap

— Page 32

Articles from *WWD* about unlocking the potential of Bergdorf Goodman. At that time (1976) Bergdorf's sales were about $38 million. In 2014 the estimate of Bergdorf's Women's store sales exceeded $700 million, with the Men's store across Fifth Avenue at roughly $80 million.

3/31/76

Betty Ford and the critics: (back row: Liz Claiborne, Shannon Rodgers, Leo Narducci (hidden), Anthony Muto, Calvin Klein, Piero Dimitri, Ann Keagy of Parsons (hidden). Front row: Donna Karan, Donald Brooks, Albert Capraro, Betty Ford, Kasper, Kay Unger, Chester Weinberg.

EYE VIEW

Parsons to Parsons

NEW YORK — "It was a coup for us to get Betty Ford to attend," said Calvin Klein, referring to the Parsons School of Design's guest of honor at Monday night's show and dinner-dance. While most of the guests were impressed with Ford's warm charisma, Peggy Butler, Anne Klein's "house model" thought this was the First Lady she could finally relate to "because we both graduated from the John Robert Powers Modelling School."

Donald Brooks was a little nervous and almost walked off the stage without presenting his Gold Thimble Award to one of the students during the fashion show. And Chip Rubinstein of Anne Klein kept a scorecard of potential designers for the Anne Klein Studio.

While most of those viewing the students' fashion show were enthusiastic about the future crop of designers, some felt the clothes were too safe and predictable. Bonwit's Lydia Sharanevych admitted, "The clothes were classically beautiful — but I had hoped to see more imagination and fantasy."

Then at 10 o'clock — hoping to find more fantasy — the movie buffs of the fashion industry slipped away to attend Academy Awards parties.

— CAROLYN GOTTFRIED

Jackie and Ira Neimark

Chip and Barbara Rubinstein

Mala Rubinstein and Oscar Kolin; Melanie Kahane with Andrew and Nena Goodman

The Fashion Award evening at Parsons featured many of the designers of that time. Liz Claiborne, Shannon Rogers, Leo Narducci, Anthony Muto, Calvin Klein. Donna Karan, David Brooks, Albert Capraro, Kasper, Kay Unger, Chester Weinberg. This was the beginning of Bergdorf Goodman's bringing in many of these designers, updating Bergdorf's fashion collections.

Articles about the assumed expansion of Bergdorf Goodman. That strategy never happened. Instead, the finances for branch stores were invested in Bergdorf Goodman on Fifth Avenue, with great success.

Also above: Meeting of Carter Hawley executives where BG was told that it was imperative to make at least one million dollar profit that year. Or else. Needless to say that figure was passed easily in the next few years, to make Bergdorf Goodman one of the most profitable retailers in the country.

Continued From Page One

Once secure as the established purveyors of fashion to an ever-constant carriage trade, these stores had their comfortable supremacy challenged in the late '60s by three things: a radically changing consumer, an economy that became increasingly difficult to read and the advent of a suddenly revitalized Bloomingdale's and a little store on 57th St. called Henri Bendel.

While Bloomingdale's and Bendel's were raking in a lot of fashion firsts and a lot of new customers at the same time, the customers themselves were becoming more individual in the way they dressed.

But for the most part, the Fifth Ave. stores failed to acknowledge the winds of change. They gravitated toward safe, matronly fashion in the face of those changes which they found difficult to comprehend. "Tasteful" continued to dominate their merchandising thrust; "exciting" rarely appeared. The cutting edge of fashion, meanwhile, had moved to the younger, more advanced customer.

Beginning about two years ago, several major top management changes gave each of these stores executives who looked at their own stores with fresh eyes. These retailers included Ira Neimark, president of Bergdorf's; John Schumacher, chairman of Bonwit's; Robert Saslow, president of Saks; Joseph Brooks, chairman of Lord & Taylor, and John Christian Jr., president of Altman's.

Some of them found operations laden with antiquated merchandising and management approaches. As they settled into their new positions, they also saw the Avenue on the verge of an image squeeze between the continuing excitement of Bloomingdale's on Lexington Ave. and 59th St. and the newly emerging trendiness of Macy's New York at Herald Square. And they are, for the most part, still struggling with the biggest problem of all — profits.

The following stories examine what has happened — and has not happened — on the Avenue in those two years.

Bergdorf Goodman

NEW YORK — In the executive offices of Bergdorf Goodman, there are several old New Yorker cartoons, framed. The Bergdorf's customer pictured in them is invariably size 16,and she looks rich and slightly stodgy.

Bergdorf's still has a lot of rich customers and its merchandise is still expensive, but the customers are no longer just stodgy. Mostly rich, maybe, but not just stodgy.

Ira Neimark, president of Bergdorf's, fervently hopes to make Bergdorf's the quality, prestige fashion store in New York. Quite ambitious, some observers feel, considering Bergdorf's went through the swinging '60s believing dumb dresses were what customers wanted.

However, Neimark has developed a staff that combines traditional Bergdorf people — conservative but with taste awareness — and new, young people — not remotely conservative but also with taste awareness.

This unusual combination seemingly works well. The store on the Plaza still retains its aura of rich respectability, but it has added flair and individuality at all price levels, thereby considerably broadening its customer appeal.

In an era when "something different or exclusive" is increasingly elusive, Bergdorf's

There are still pockets of blandness, but Bergdorf's is beginning to generate excitement.

has managed to corner a little of both, due primarily to its young buyers and merchandisers who hustle like a bunch of blackbirds on a fall day to unearth unknowns with something special. Obviously, they have been given a lot of leeway by management; and, as Neimark says, "Price is secondary."

Some of the resources they have found:

• Andrea Brava Maza, discovered in a small Left Bank shop in Paris. Bergdorf's started off with about 350 of her simple dresses in beautiful cottons ($60 to $80 retail) and sold 250 in one season.

• Covent Garden Dance Centre in London, where Bergdorf's found the school's dancewear shop, complete with leotards and leg warmers, and gathered together the professional merchandise for a little shop on Bergdorf's sixth floor.

• Charvet, maker of custom women's shirts in Paris, special because of the lovely fabrics and painstaking details — beautifully finished shirttails, gentle yokes, tiny self-ties and small silk cords woven into button-shaped cufflinks.

Bergdorf's also has brought in a lot of European designers who are new to the store and has expanded areas where it has discovered great consumer acceptance.

Krizia has been enlarged because the

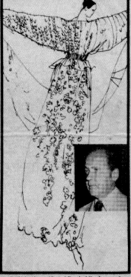

Ira Neimark, president of Bergdorf Goodman, and a lace skirt and loose sweater top ($4.25) by Krizia, a designer who has a strong following at the store. An early window on the fall collection drew such a response the store had to place a reorder before the first order was delivered.

store found it has a contemporary customer who travels a lot, likes relaxed, easy clothes and sportswear that isn't tough or tailored and buys Krizia because it's all of that. The store, for instance, put Krizia's fall merchandise ($90 to $300) in its Fifth Ave. windows in April and had to place a reorder before the first order was even delivered.

Again, early spring windows of Andrea Odacini's heavy crepe de chine dresses — not at all classic in design and priced between $900 and $1,000 — sold 34 of the dresses in one week.

Similarly, while the store always had an excellent fur business, it had been heavy into traditional furs. Last year, though, Bergdorf's bought 50 of Fendi's contemporary

furs and found a customer for them. This year, it's buying close to three times as much and also is adding St. Laurent furs for men and women.

Bergdorf's is adding a lot more than that this fall — Basile and Armani for the first time, a shop for Chanel ready-to-wear, a Bottega Veneta shop for handbags and accessories, Trussardi's handbags and suede ready-to-wear, Mario Valentino for the first time, a Cerruti shop, Porta International (classic sportswear made in Hong Kong and exclusive at Bergdorf's) and Gil Aimber's entire line, including some exclusives for the store.

Last spring, Bergdorf's brought French couture back to the store. Of the 30 pieces bought for a major fashion presentation, 17 were sold before the show at prices close to what they would retail for in Paris.

This fall, the store bought approximately 50 French couture pieces, including Dior, St. Laurent, Givenchy and Chanel. In addition, the store bought 12 pieces of Italian couture from Andre Laug and Muriel Grateau.

Since Neimark took over Bergdorf's in March 1975, the Fifth Ave. store's volume has been growing at a rate of about $2,500,000 a year. The flagship store did about $36,500,000 in 1975, reportedly hit $39-million in 1976 and is expected to do between $41,500,000 and $42 million in 1977.

However, there are those who wonder if Bergdorf's is overextending itself in imports and regard this fall as the acid test of whether a big import business can be profitable.

During the 2½ year period Neimark has been at the store, the look of the operation as well as its entire merchandising philosophy has changed. Bergdorf's main floor was given almost an immediate upbeat when Neimark moved the cosmetics department from its outpost in the back to the front of the door. Subsequently, an elegant Fendi handbag and accessories boutique took another front spot on the main floor, along with a tiny section of Fendi rtw.

Elsewhere in the store, departments were reorganized to either project certain underdeveloped areas or to effect more logical placement.

The sixth floor became the Sixth Sense, a repository for of-the-minute contemporary fashion. It is here that a lot of the discoveries — unknowns or "little people" — end up.

In the process of all this reorganization, the store's floors have become more fluid and inviting. There are still pockets of blandness, but by and large, Bergdorf's is beginning to generate the kind of excitement that marks it as a store to be watched.

Bonwit Teller

Bonwit Teller has been called an enigma by observers. While the store gets high marks for a willingness to project fashion with a lack of focus about who it is. In trying to be forward, the store has gone after newness, sources say, without building on some of the categories it already has.

The store has quality merchandise that should be developed further rather than jam-

WWD survey of the Fifth Avenue stores in 1978 with positive marks for Bergdorf compared to the other stores.

Eugenia Sheppard in 1977 writing about the couture of Saint Laurent, Dior and Givenchy arriving at Bergdorf. This generated attention from designers and customers.

WOMEN'S WEAR DAILY, WEDNESDAY, MAY 17, 1978

ALL IN THE FAMILY: "They — the New York inner circle — gathered Monday for a special evening in the new $450,000 restaurant, Le Chantilly, on East 57th St., which is owned by **Paul Dessibourg** (ex-Cote Basque and La Grenouille) and co-owned by **Ronald Chanus**, who is also chef, ex-Veau d'Or. There was **Prince Rupert Loewenstein**, who blew rather smelly cigar smoke across the table at the Perrier-drinking girls — **Isabel Eberstadt**, in glorious blown hairdo — **Annette Reed** in lacy blouse, on her way to Mexico and just back from a trip with **Robert Redford** in the interest of bird conservation — **Helene David-Weill**, without her husband, Michele, who has the measles — bubbling **Genevieve Faure** — **Geraldine Stutz**, who was the last to arrive, wearing a light plum satin dress with drawstring neckline — **Brando Brandolini**, back from his son's graduation in Texas — architect **Jacquin Robinson** — **Sam Spiegel**, who has a new project up his sleeve — **Egon Von Furstenberg**, who has written a new book on (you guessed it) how to dress for "The Power Look." — **Louis Jourdan**, who sang after dinner to his hostess, **Francoise de la Renta**, who was just off the Concorde after Ideacomo in Milan, and Paris.

Oscar de la Renta, also in from Ideacomo, was admiring **Ralph Lauren's** initialed evening pumps, which came up too high in back, and were worn with gray flannels and tweed jacket. **Eugenia Corraf** sat next to some of the younger set, namely **John Radziwill**. And there was **Bob Silvers** — New York Review of Books' **Grace Dudley**, gracefully dodging pieces of bread thrown by **Andre Oliver** — **Chessy Rayner**, without her husband, Bill, who was at the Rhode Island School of Design — **Nan Kempner**, who lifted her skirts to show dotted black lace stockings, and explained her husband's absence with "Tommy is working" — **Giancarlo Giametti**, wearing pink glasses and narrow Punky necktie — **Valentino**, looking elegant and reserved, as always.

Mica and **Ahmet Ertegun**, who co-hosted the dinner, selected the menu of foie gras a la Cosmos, saddle of veal, carrots, celery and turnip from California and a mushy strawberry mousse. The wines were a white Chateau de Vire 1976, a red Chateau Simard 1973 St. Emillion and a Taittinger 1970 champagne.

John Christian (above left); Bob Benzio and Ellin Saltzman (above)

ChicLee Mollis

Sheila and Richard Schwartz

WWD photos by TONY PALMIERI

Mayor Ed Koch and Shirley Goodman

IT'S NOT FIT WEATHER...: "The smartest thing I did was to wear long underwear," said **Ellin Saltzman**, Saks Fifth Avenue's vice-president. She was part of the familiar mix of retailers, manufacturers and politicians huddled under the big yellow and white striped tent at Gracie Mansion in New York, the Ladies clutching their furs as protection against the cold and high winds. The annual FIT Scholarship dinner-dance had moved uptown this year because of construction underway downtown at the school.

"Let's try and look warm," said Bloomingdale's **Marvin Traub** as he posed for the photographers.

"He looks better real," said **Stanley Love**, as he viewed **Mayor Ed Koch** in person for the first time.

There were the usual pre-dinner speeches, including one from Gov. **Hugh Carey**, who chided the industry "to do better with rain gear" that would stay dry in a downpour like the one last Sunday. Carey then sat down and had a tete-a-tete with the politicians' favorite, **Abe Schrader**.

— CAROLYN GOTTFRIED

Sol and Rosalind Chaikin

Gov. Hugh Carey and Abe Schrader

Ira and Pat Neimark

One of the many Woman's Wear news articles including Jackie and me representing recognition of the rise of Bergdorf Goodman becoming the leading fashion retailer.

Because of Bergdorf Goodman promoting French couture, Jackie and I were honored at formal dinner at Versailles.

40   *Style*   THE NEW YORK TIMES, SUNDAY, JULY 30, 1978

It Was Just a Little Dinner Party at Versailles

By BERNADINE MORRIS

Grace Mirabella chats with Louise Rouet, top; Philippe Venet with Nan Kempner and Lynn Wyatt, center; Givenchy and Gerald Van der Kemp, right.

Jackie Nemark, above; Estée Lauder and Tatiana Liberman.

The introduction of Fendi Furs and Handbags in one location exclusively at Bergdorf Goodman got the attention of designers not only in Italy, but France and America as well. The press regarding the couture at Bergdorf Goodman was overwhelming.

Bergdorf Goodman was included in all major fashion events. The Metropolitan Museum's great fashion shows started in the 1970s by Diana Vreeland, sponsored by Fith Avenue retailers, with Pat Buckley and Bill Blass on the receiving line, had grown into a major New York fashion event.

Bergdorf Goodman's promotion of Lacroix in 1987
introducing his newest collection at the Crystal Palace
in NY was a sensation. With all the important society
people as well as the press, it was a spectacular success.

This is a sample of correspondence received via Princess Diana's lady in waiting regarding Bergdorf Goodman keeping the princess informed about fashion news and events.

Letter from Princess Diana' Secretary

BUCKINGHAM PALACE

From: Lady-in-Waiting to H.R.H. The Princess of Wales

28th October 1986

Dear Mr Neimark,

The Princess of Wales has asked me to thank you very much for your letter, together with a copy of the New York Times Magazine with the article about Bergdorf Goodman.

Her Royal Highness was grateful to you for sending this and was most interested to read about the store. The Princess asks me to send you and your wife her best wishes and to say how much she enjoyed meeting you at the British Fashion Banquet earlier this month.

Yours sincerely,

Anne Beckwith-Smith

Miss A. Beckwith-Smith

Mr. I. Neimark

Parties with our family, plus other business friends. Being honored at various events such as The Denver Jewish Hospital, as well as Bergdorf Goodman receiving the CFD Award. Plus BG having a $250,000 day with a Donna Karan Event.

Karan has $250,000 day at Bergdorf's

NEW YORK — Donna Karan did more than $250,000 at Bergdorf Goodman Tuesday, the opening day of her newly expanded boutique at the store, according to Ira Neimark, chairman.

When Bergdorf's introduced Karan last year, first-day sales of her detail collection were roughly $100,000. Last year, volume was $50,000 on each of the two following days, bringing the three-day total to $200,000.

The business was strong enough during the last year to prompt Bergdorf's to expand Karan's 250-square-foot boutique to about 500 square feet.

When the new space opened Tuesday, the fall collection was featured with a trunk show. Orders were being taken for August delivery.

Article in 1986 Fashion Network

MAN OF THE YEAR: IRA NEIMARK--RETAILING

IRA NEIMARK, CHAIRMAN

IN FORTY YEARS HE WENT 300 FEET FROM A STOCK BOY AT BONWIT TELLER TO CHAIRMAN OF THE QUINTESSENTIAL SPECIALTY STORE, BERGDORF GOODMAN. HE HAS NO COLLEGE DEGREE. HE NEVER LEARNED RETAILING FROM A GRADUATE SCHOOL. HE DIDN'T JOIN THE TRAINING SQUAD AT MACY'S OR BLOOMINGDALE'S. HE NEVER OWNED A STORE.

IRA NEIMARK IS THE HORATIO ALGER OF RETAILING. HE IS URBANE, OPINIONATED, STYLISH IN DEMEANOR, SOFT SPOKEN, A STICKLER FOR PERFECTION AND A WORKA- HOLIC. AT THE ZENITH OF HIS RETAIL- ING CAREER HE PRESIDES LIKE A MANDAR- IN OVER THE AMERICAN RETAILING DIADEM. IN A DISASTROUS YEAR FOR MOST STORES HE DELIVERED AN OUTSTANDING BOTTOM LINE WITH A DRAMATIC INCREASE IN VOL- UME. THIS RELENTLESS QUEST FOR SUCC- ESS COMBINED WITH A KEEN VISION FOR THE FUTURE IS THE STUFF THAT MADE THE GREAT MERCHANT PRINCES OF THIS CENTURY LIKE STANLEY MARCUS AND ANDREW GOOD- MAN. HE IS THE "MAN OF THE YEAR" IN RETAILING AND THERE IS NO CLOSE COM- PETITOR.

WILLIAM M. HOLMES, BONWIT'S PRESIDENT, DURING THE '40'S WAS NEIMARK'S FIRST RABBI IN BUSINESS. HOLMES GAVE THE YOUNG STOCK BOY RECOGNITION AND A SCHOLARSHIP TO COLUMBIA UNIVERSITY. AFTER WW II NEIMARK'S RETAILING CAR- EER BLOSSOMED IN NEW ENGLAND: FIRST AT A STODGY RHODE ISLAND SPECIALTY CHAIN, GLADDING'S ("I ROSE TO GMM OF THE STORE AND GODFATHER OF THE GLADDING'S CHILDREN AND THEY NEVER HAD A JEW IN MANAGEMENT BEFORE...") AND LATER HE JOINED G. FOX WHERE HE WORKED AS GMM UNDER THE LEGENDARY MERCHANT EMPRESS, BEATRICE AUBERACH FOX ("SHE WAS A GREAT RETAILER AND SUPERB PERSON OF GREAT TASTE...I LEFT WHEN THE MAY CO. TOOK OVER.").

PHIL HAWLEY, CHAIRMAN OF THE BELEAGUR- ED CARTER, HAWLEY, HALE CHAIN THAT OWNS BERGDORF'S, HIRED NEIMARK AWAY FROM THE MAIDEN AUNT OF FIFTH AVENUE, B. ALTMAN'S, IN 1975. "I KNEW HAWLEY FROM HIS DAYS AS GMM OF THE BROADWAY AND HE OFFERED ME THE JOB WITH A CARTE BLANCHE TO RUN THE STORE AND TO DEVE- LOP ITS PROFITABILITY," NEIMARK SAYS.

IN '86 BERGDORF'S WILL DO $ 115 MILLION IN SALES IN 144,000 SQUARE FEET OF SPACE. WHEN HE TOOK OVER THE 85 YEAR OLD DOWAGER OF FIFTH AVENUE IT DID $ 30 MILLION IN 100,000 SQUARE FEET. "I HAVE THE HIGHEST REGARD FOR HAWLEY'S COURAGE AND LEADERSHIP AND THE UTMOST RESPECT FOR ANDREW GOODMAN'S METICULOUS GOOD TASTE," HE SAYS.

BERGDORF'S DOES 50% OF ITS VOLUME WITH 10% OF ITS CHARGE CUSTOMERS. THE STORE ROMANCES ITS HIGH ROLLERS AND IS EX- PANDING ITS BUSINESS THROUGH ITS CAT- ALOGS WITH ITS NEW CUSTOMERS. NEIMARK KNOWS ALMOST EVERY SALESPERSON BY NAME AND MEETS WITH THEM AT SPECIAL "HYPE" SESSIONS WEEKLY. THE STORE'S GROWTH HAS BEEN ORCHESTRATED THROUGH A MASTERFUL INCREASE OF SELLING SPACE, THE ADDITION OF AN ESCALATOR, A CAREFUL RENOVATION OF THE FIFTH AVENUE WINDOWS AND FRONT, A PLANNED EXPANSION OF ITS "SPECIAL" DESIGNER COLLECTIONS, THE VIGOROUS GROWTH OF ITS MAIN FLOOR ACCESSORIES BUSINESS, A REMARKABLE $ 2,500 PER SQUARE FOOT IN COSMETIC SALES, A DIP- LOMATIC RELOCATION OF THE DELMAN SHOE CONCESSION AND AN ONGOING EMPHASIS ON BUILDING RELATIONSHIPS WITH ITS QUALITY VENDORS, "MY HANDSHAKE WITH A VENDOR IS GOLDEN," NEIMARK REMARKS ABOUT HIS OBSESSION WITH THE DETAILS OF EVERY "DEAL" WITH DESIGNERS AND MANUFACTURERS.

IN '87 THE STORE WILL ACHIEVE $ 1,000 IN SALES PER SQUARE FOOT. IT WILL BE NEIMARK'S CROWNING ACHIEVEMENT. ###

ALAN G. MILLSTEIN, EDITOR AND PUBLISHER
FASHION NETWORK, 220 E. 57th. St., NYC 10022/212-752-5611

National Jewish Hospital dinner honoring Ira Neimark

Bergdorf Goodman's India Party

THE NEW YORK TIMES, WEDNESDAY, NOVEMBER 27, 1985

Indian Elegance at a Party at Bergdorf's

By BERNADINE MORRIS

FOR the next two weeks, Bergdorf Goodman will be suffused with merchandise from India, from quilts so elegantly made they can double as wall hangings to men's cummerbunds and ties in, of course, saris. The saris are not the kind you drape yourself, a challenge even to Western women who have spent some time in India. Rather, sari fabrics, glimmering with gold threads, have been made into evening dresses by Victor Costa. At least one was worn to the black-tie dinner party Monday night called "A Celebration of India" that opened Bergdorf's first storewide promotion and the first devoted to a specific country.

"I'm enjoying it, it's a fun dress," said Linda Laxus, whose husband, William, owns a steel mill. "We have a lot of black-tie invitations and I thought it would be a nice change from the usual evening dress."

Mrs. Laxus's sari-based dress was in green and gold silk and was one of four Costa styles sold before the promotion opened.

"We put some of the merchandise out on the floor as it arrived," said

Hostess applies dot to forehead of Edith McBean, left; fur-trimmed silk brocade suit by Victor Costa, $1,595, above.

In quilts, ties and sari dresses a celebration of fabric, fashion.

Dawn Mello, Bergdorf's president. "There was such a terrific demand, we had to take it off sale or we wouldn't have had anything in the store."

Mr. Costa, who makes evening dresses in Dallas in the $350 to $500 range, was inspired by the success of his sari dresses to start a higher-priced division called Costa Couture. Prices will range from $800 to $2,000.

Arnold Scaasi is familiar with couture clothes, having added ready-to-wear to his repertory just a few seasons ago. For this occasion, he made bouffant strapless dresses from ivory-colored saris woven with gold thread and added red or royal blue satin jackets. They sell for $5,000. He arrived at the party with Kimberly and Jonathan Farkas. She was wearing a short dress with a long black peplum and puff pleat skirt over narrow black pants.

"Kimberly asked me what she should wear and I told her Diana Vreeland said, 'Pink is the navy blue of India,' so she chose this one," Mr. Scaasi said.

"I had a Nehru jacket once by Valentino and it was great," said Mr. Farkas, scanning the store's main floor scattered with men and women from the United States and India dressed in Indian garb. "I wonder if I should get another."

Partygoers entered the store under a canopy of brilliantly colored umbrellas held aloft by men in white linen tunics with red cummerbunds. Women in saris offered each female guest a tikka, the dot worn on the forehead, in colors to match individual dresses. Large platters of marigolds on the floors and counters helped set the scene.

Guests then passed through the receiving line consisting of Ira Neimark, Bergdorf's chairman; Miss Mello, in a gold lamé Costa dress, and

Jeweled bags and shoes of Indian silks, above; Bina Ramani, left, chats with Jackie Brummund in turban she wrapped herself, right.

Dailey Pattee, co-chairman of the evening and president of the Women's Committee of the New York Zoological Society. The society received the entire proceeds of the $190 tickets, said Mrs. Pattee, who was wearing a black dress by Jacqueline de Ribes "because a sari doesn't work very well when you've just had a baby," she said.

Among the honored guests were the Maharajah of Jaipur; his wife, the Maharani, in a green sari, and their daughter, Princess Diya, who wore pink. Also present were Lalitha and Natarajan Krishnan. He is the chief of the Indian mission to the United Nations.

Fashion designers who turned up to inspect Bergdorf's view of India were Bill Blass, Gianfranco Ferré and Issey Miyake. Mr. Ferré said he was returning to the store the next day to do his Christmas shopping and promised to attend the India party at the Metropolitan Museum of Art next month. Mr. Miyake's clothes in Indian fabrics were displayed on the main floor. Kenneth Jay Lane announced he was opening a shop next week on Columbus Avenue and was spending Christmas in India. "I always do," he said. "Where else is there?"

After drinks, the crowd of more than 300 rode the escalators to the seventh floor, where a buffet supper by Remember Basil was served. The food included tandoori chicken, leg of lamb and an assortment of chutneys. The Indian beer was widely admired.

"It is a crash course in Indian culture," said Mr. Scaasi, who said he was familiar with the fabrics because "not a month goes by that a woman doesn't bring me a sari and ask me to turn it into a dress."

Miss Mello was so pleased with the enthusiasm of the guests that she said she would have Indian merchandise in the store every year before Christmas. "The craftsmanship is overwhelming and the atmosphere is a little like Italy after World War II, with cottage industries," she said. "I think it will grow, like Italian design, and we will grow with it."

The New York Times/William E. Sauro and Bill Cunningham

Geoffrey Beene's Party in Vienna

Left to right: Ira Neimark, Jackie Neimark,
Bernadine Morris, Geoffrey
Beene, HelenO'Hagen, Dawn Mello

Party in 1983 celebrating Berdotf Goodman's new
escalators

AT BERGDORF'S

Snacking among the clothes

The fifth-floor buffet

Carol Phillips

Andree Putman

Power on: Ira Neimark, Carla Fendi,
Aldo Pinto; James Galanos surveys the
scene (above left)

Photos by TONY PALMIERI

Mission accomplished

The breathless journey

Giorgio Sant'Angelo

Louis dell'Olio, Donna Karan

A hardhat guide

Bergdorf Goodman Chanel fashion show

WOMEN'S WEAR DAILY, TUESDAY, SEPTEMBER 17, 1983

EYE — Tuning in on Chanel

Kitty D'Alessio   Carroll Petrie   Alain Wertheimer and Dolores Bosshard   Anne Johnson   Kathleen Hearst   Anne Bass

Betsy Kaiser and Barbara Bancroft

Renee Monell and Nina Griscom   Mary Meehan   Brigitte Wertheimer and Ira Neimark   Josephine Wilson   Ivana Trump and Cathy Tankoos

NEW YORK — On Monday, the lightly tanned Ladies settled down to the serious business of shopping for clothes. They began at the Bergdorf Goodman show of Chanel boutique and couture, shown for the first time in many years in the United States, to benefit the School of American Ballet. "I consider something new something that is three or four years old," said co-chairwoman **Betsy Kaiser.** "The Chanel

suits are still sensational. The problem is keeping your weight down so you can wear these clothes for 20 years," added Kaiser, admiring the Chanel long shirtwaist dress. **Anne Bass** said she'd been in Europe this summer, where she'd bought clothes by **Saint Laurent** and **Ungaro,** and still is interested in Chanel for evening.

— JOYCE WILSON

Photos by GEORGE CHINSEE

IN MEMORIAM: Francoise de la Renta will be remembered tonight at a service at the Church of Saint Vincent Ferrer in New York. **Zubin Mehta** will conduct members of the New York Philharmonic, and eulogies will be given by **Guy de Rothschild** in French and **Henry Kissinger** in English. **Oscar de la Renta,** who invited close friends and professional associates of his late wife, also has arranged for simple flowers at the church. After the 6:30 p.m. service, **Ahmet** and **Mica Ertegun** will have a dinner for 35 of those attending.

The opening of Guerlain's first shop in the United States

Bergdorf's makes room for Guerlain shop

NEW YORK — Ira Neimark, chairman and chief executive officer of Bergdorf Goodman, will strike another blow for exclusivity in early April when he opens a Guerlain shop on the store's first floor. According to Neimark and Michel Vincent, president of Guerlain, Inc., Bergdorf's will be the only store with a Guerlain shop, and the only one to carry Guerlain's Issima skin care line, now sold only in the international market.

The Guerlain Boutique, to be called Guerlain at Bergdorf's, is the centerpiece of a renovation and expansion of the store's cosmetics department. By next spring, when construction is completed, cosmetics space will be increased 50 percent, with total cosmetics volume expected to increase by a similar amount, one industry source said. More lines, as yet undetermined, will be added, the placement of other lines will be improved and treatment rooms will be built, Neimark said. The expansion is part of a step-by-step overhaul of the entire store.

Guerlain at Bergdorf's will be in the oval rotunda in front of three elevators facing the 58th

"It's recognition of the effort they are making to look different, to be different."
— Michel Vincent

Street entrance. The space is now occupied by fragrances, which will move to the area now housing the Hermès boutique. That shop will move out of the store in early spring, according to Dawn Mello, president.

Cosmetics will also be expanded into the area adjacent to the Hermès boutique not now used for selling.

Neimark said fixturing and decor of the new areas will be "dramatic within the taste level of Bergdorf Goodman." Construction in the fragrance area of a miniature version of the fountain outside the Plaza Hotel is being considered. One source estimated the first-floor renovation would cost one-fifth of the amount being spent on the entire store renovation, a figure Neimark placed at $15 million.

The 400-square-foot Guerlain shop will be modeled on the Guerlain shop on the Champs d'Ely-

"We're first going to make a success of the venture with Bergdorf Goodman before thinking of rolling."
— Vincent

sees, one of four Guerlain shops in Paris. It will contain four marble counters, one in each corner of the rotunda. Although details have not been completely worked out, Vincent said at least two of the counters will be used for the treatment line, with the remainder of the space devoted to fragrances. The center of the floor, which now holds a fragrance bar, will be empty, Mello said. The boutique will quadruple Guerlain's space at the store. Although Neimark declined to comment on his projections for sales at the boutique, one source said they are expected to exceed $1,000 per square foot.

According to Vincent, discussions between Guerlain and Bergdorf's have been going on for about two years. Bergdorf's was an appropriate choice for the boutique because Neimark's concern with obtaining exclusive merchandise corresponds to Guerlain's objective to stay at the extreme upper end of the market, Vincent said. "It's recognition of the effort they are making to look different, to be different," he said.

Some of the most recent examples of Neimark's quest for exclusivity are the construction of the Musée des Arts Decoratifs home furnishings shop, which opened Oct. 26, and an Angela Cummings jewelry shop, planned for next year. Neimark also demonstrated that concern in June when Bergdorf's said it would no longer carry Halston ready-to-wear and cosmetics after the designer signed a licensing deal with J.C. Penney for the Halston III apparel line.

Vincent and Neimark said the contract between Bergdorf's and Guerlain does not set a time limit for the exclusivity. They would not discuss the financial stipulations of the contract. Vincent declined to predict when the treatment line would be expanded to other stores. "We're first going to make a success of the venture with Bergdorf Goodman before thinking of rolling out," Vincent said.

Issima is the best-selling of three Guerlain treatment lines, none of which have ever been sold here. It accounts for about 20 percent of Guerlain's worldwide treatment volume. Its 12 stockkeeping units include four foundations, day and night creams, eye and neck creams, a body cream, ampoules, a mask and a cleanser. Prices have not been firmly set, but will probably range from about

A sketch of the planned Guerlain shop at Bergdorf Goodman

$27.50 for the foundation to $95 for the ampoules.

The products are aimed at women over 30 and are based on an ingredient called Hydrolastine, a combination of elastine, silicon collagen and lactic acid. They were developed by Guerlain's research lab in Chartres and were launched in Europe in 1980.

"It's a direct attack on La Prairie," Vincent said, referring to Jacqueline Cochran's high-priced, narrowly distributed treatment line.

Promotional plans for the line have not been completed, but will include heavy sampling, said Nick Jordan, Guerlain's vice president of sales. There will be skin care clinics, either in groups or on a one-to-one basis, and counter consultants will keep a card on each customer. Jordan believes the line has the potential for a large mail order business at Bergdorf's.

The Guerlain shop will also exclusively sell several fragrances now sold only in Europe — Vol de Nuit, Eau Cologne du Coq, Eau de Fleurs de Cedrat, Eau de Guerlain and Apres L'Ondee. There will also be line extensions in the Jicky fragrance line.

— NORMA SENTO

Ira Neimark (above), Guerlain's Issima eye cream, Michel Vincent (below)

Women's Wear Daily Louise Esterhazy page

Bergdorf Goodman's Krizia fashion show at the Museum
of Natural History

My letter inviting Princess Diana to visit Bergdorf
Goodman

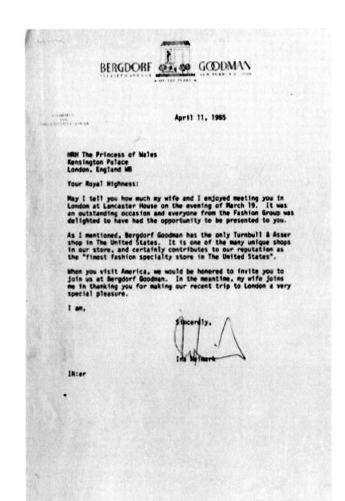

BERGDORF GOODMAN

April 11, 1985

HRH The Princess of Wales
Kensington Palace
London, England W8

Your Royal Highness:

May I tell you how much my wife and I enjoyed meeting you in
London at Lancaster House on the evening of March 19. It was
an outstanding occasion and everyone from the Fashion Group was
delighted to have had the opportunity to be presented to you.

As I mentioned, Bergdorf Goodman has the only Turnbull & Asser
shop in The United States. It is one of the many unique shops
in our store, and certainly contributes to our reputation as
the "finest fashion specialty store in The United States".

When you visit America, we would be honored to invite you to
join us at Bergdorf Goodman. In the meantime, my wife joins
me in thanking you for making our recent trip to London a very
special pleasure.

I am,

Sincerely,

Ira Neimark

IN:ar

Montana Fashion show

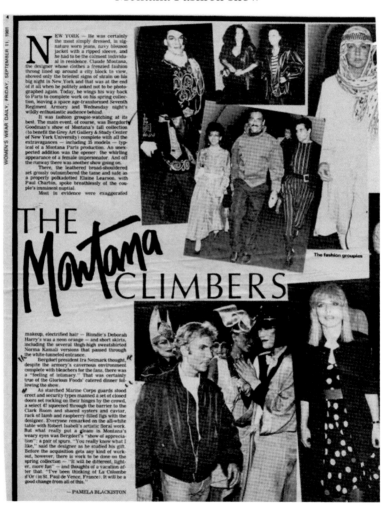

WOMEN'S WEAR DAILY, FRIDAY, SEPTEMBER 11, 1981

NEW YORK — He was certainly the most simply dressed, in signature worn jeans, navy blouson jacket with a ripped sleeve, and he had to be the calmest individual in residence. Claude Montana, the designer whose clothes a frenzied fashion throng lined up around a city block to view, showed only the briefest signs of strain on his big night in New York and that was at the end of it all when he politely asked not to be photographed again. Today, he wings his way back to Paris to complete work on his spring collection, leaving a space age-transformed Seventh Regiment Armory and Wednesday night's wildly enthusiastic audience behind.

It was fashion groupie-watching at its best. The main event, of course, was Bergdorf Goodman's show of Montana's fall collection (to benefit the Grey Art Gallery & Study Center of New York University) complete with all the extravagances — including 35 models — typical of a Montana Paris production. An unexpected addition was the opener: the whirling appearance of a female impersonator. And off the runway there was another show going on.

There, the leathered broad-shouldered set grossly outnumbered the tame and safe as a properly polkadotted Elaine Learson, with Paul Charbin, spoke breathlessly of the couple's imminent nuptial.

Most in evidence were exaggerated

THE Montana CLIMBERS

The fashion groupies

makeup, electrified hair — Blondie's Deborah Harry's was a neon orange — and short skirts, including the several thigh-high sweatshirted Norma Kamali versions that passed through the white-tunneled entrance.

Bergdorf president Ira Neimark thought, despite the armory's cavernous environment complete with bleachers for the fans, there was a "feeling of intimacy." That was certainly true of the Glorious Foods' catered dinner following the show.

As starched Marine Corps guards stood erect and security types manned a set of closed doors set rocking on their hinges by the crowd, a select 47 squeezed through the barrier to the Clark Room and shared oysters and caviar, rack of lamb and raspberry-filled figs with the designer. Everyone remarked on the all-white table with Robert Isabell's artistic floral work. But what really put a gleam in Montana's weary eyes was Bergdorf's "show of appreciation": a pair of spurs. "You really know what I like," said the designer as he studied his gift. Before the acquisition gets any kind of workout, however, there is work to be done on the spring collection — "It will be different, lighter, more fun" — and thoughts of a vacation after that. "I've been thinking of La Colombe d'Or (in St. Paul de Vence, France). It will be a good change from all of this."

— PAMELA BLACKISTON

Fendi Fashion show at the Pulitzer Fountain

Ungaro fashion show at Bergdorf Goodman

EYE.

Victor Skrebneski and Emanuel Ungaro

Grey Watkins

WWD photos by DUSTIN PITTMAN

Jane Neimark

Cristina de Caraman Goldsmith, Catherine de Limur

Suzanne Pascal, Francoise de la Renta

Jay Rossbach, Arnold Aronson

Carolyn Amory

Eva Malmstrom

Pauline Trigere, Jim Wagnon

Joan Fontaine

UNGARO UNVEILED: Bergdorf Goodman premiered its **Ungaro** boutique in New York Tuesday night with a cocktail reception in the store for a group of the designer's customers and friends, and some who were a bit of both. "We really have an international woman," said Ungaro, looking slim but certainly not shaven, "so we must have a home here." The sleek beige boutique, designed by **Norwood Oliver** and the Bergdorf's staff, was a sea of Ungaro's lush velvets and gilded embroideries, worn by his customers. "Just look at me from the waist up," said **Grey Watkins,** "since only my blouse is Ungaro."

Then, Wednesday morning, at another Bergdorf's showing of the Ungaro collection, to benefit the Museum of the City of New York, the first brisk fall weather produced many layered looks among the Ladies' fashion finery. Front-row seated **Lee Radziwill** said she had "bought Italian" for her wardrobe purchases thus far this season. Patting the fur-lined Fendi coat she did not remove until halfway through the show, she said, "It feels terrific."

Hannah Pakula said she'd invested in an Ungaro challis even before the store's event. **Jean Tailer,** in a new **Adolfo** suit, described New York's social scene as "unbelievably busy lately — like some ancient decadent city before the fall."

Also among those present were **Hilary Geary** and **Nina Griscom,** who singled out the sophisticated black evening clothes near the finale as their Ungaro favorites. **Mary Meehan,** whose fall purchases included Versace, **Michaele Vollbracht** and **Calvin Klein,** nonetheless complained, "They haven't come in from the manufacturers yet. Now I have to go out and buy them directly from the stores."

— SALLY RINARD and JANE F. LANE

FOR ART'S SAKE: It couldn't have been any plainer if they'd worn signs on their backs or spoke through bullhorns. What separated the women from the girls at the opening of Saks Fifth Avenue's Adam L. Gimbel SoHo-esque Gallery in New York Tuesday evening were chunky, formidable green glass necklaces by **Suzanne Pascal,** the exhibiting impressionist sculptor, worn by such guests as **Serena Felt** and **Patricia Kluge.**

Pauline Trigere shook her fist at the ineffable strength of the artist's displayed heads and figures with brave, often punished expressions, noting of the 13½-foot stainless steel Man and Woman, "I fell in love with the pair. I'm not sure I have the place for it. But I have the funds" — $44,000. "I want to put them in my backyard. We'll see. They are Adam and Eve or something."

Ellin Saltzman eyed the grand space enviously while a vivacious Pascal, the only practicing artist in the difficult hammer-and-chisel glass medium, recounted how **Prince Charles** marveled at her jewelry at the Royal Ballet. "I was with **Dr. Armand Hammer,** who then commissioned a piece as a wedding present to the Prince of Wales and Diana," she said.

And nobody at the party, it seemed, missed the linen shop which the gallery had replaced.

— CHRISTOPHER PETKANAS

Bergdorf's Armani fashion show, 1980 at the Prometheus
Fountain, Radio City

Bergdorf Goodman's magnificent main floor

Jackie and Geoffrey Beene celebrating

Eugenia Sheppard honored at Maxims, Paris with Princess Grace of Monaco

Fair Post's Eugenia Sheppard is surrounded by, left to right, Mark Bohan, Philippe Heurtault, Prince Albert, Princess Grace and Princess Caroline.

Rtw showings attract top US retailers

Bergorf Goodman continued its sales and profit growth. Ira Neimark is promoted, in addition to being the CEO of Bergdorf Goodman, appointed Vice President of General Cinema and Merchandise Advisor to Neiman Marcus

Because Dawn Mello and Ira Neimark were influential in convincing Donna Karan to open her own business, Bergdorf Goodman was able to arrange her exclusive fashion shows at Bergdorf.

Dinner honoring Ira Neimark
It was the responsibility—and honor—for a CEO to
participate in important charitable events

Bergdorf's business kept growing at 15 percent each year.

Because of Bergdorf Goodman's fashion designer strategy, sales increase dramatically for the store. This strategy also increased the visibility of the designers to the degree that many became brands. This allowed Designers as brands to open their own regular price shops, open discount shops, license their lines and many other advantages.

WWD article about qualities of a perfect CEO;
happy to be included with other perfect CEOs

What Makes the Perfect Retail CEO?

Unlike other ceos,
Finkelstein almost has
an excess of candidates
who could be considered
for the top spot.

After intense promotion of Fendi at Bergdorf Goodman, BG made Fendi a famous brand, allowing them to open many of their own shops.

FINALE

Below, the Vanderbilt mansion: where Bergdorf
Goodman stands today

A Final Reflection

And so, this is the story of how I retired happily and successfully and lived to be 100, or close to it, since I'm not quite there yet.

Retiring to enjoy the rest of one's life is the reward a person is entitled to after a lifetime of, as I have written—with a bit of help—the pinball of life bouncing in the right direction.

There are times, of course, in the pinball theory, that the ball will bounce in the wrong direction. Good luck and timing helped me at the lower point of my business career. Determination and persistency seem to be the combination of tools that got my career back on track.

As for health, that seems to be in the lap of the gods.

However, the medical profession has made great strides during my long lifetime. To help the gods help me, I've been able to make frequent visits to my doctor any time I didn't feel 100 percent.

Hopefully, what I've written will be helpful to the reader of this memoir.

With my best wishes for a long, successful and healthy life, I am sincerely yours.

Index